# GETTING STARTED

The ability to draw the human head and figure is an essential skill for every artist. The clear, easy-to-follow instructions presented here will be a valuable asset to you. By using these techniques, you can rapidly improve your skills, and gain new confidence in your ability to draw people. We'll cover all of the essentials, including structure and proportions, but we'll place an emphasis on the basic principles that will give you the tools you need to draw figures in a variety of poses. Let's start with the features of the face. The eyes, nose, and mouth begin with simple shapes, which will help you to draw each feature convincingly.

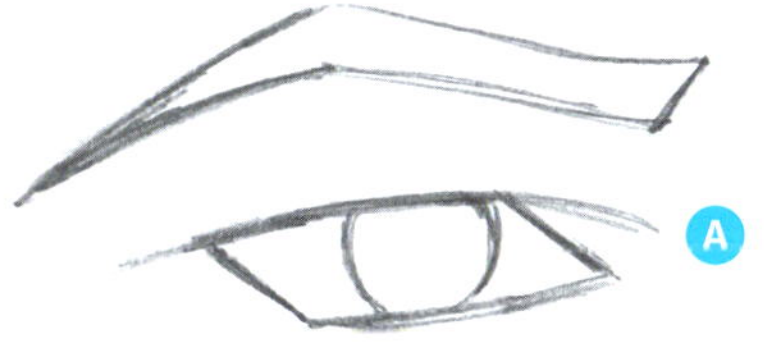


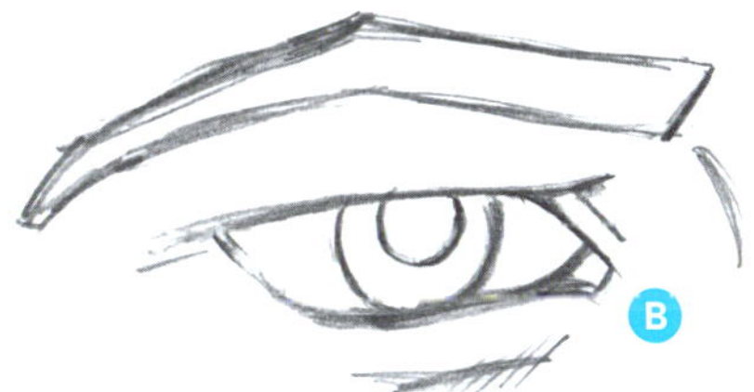


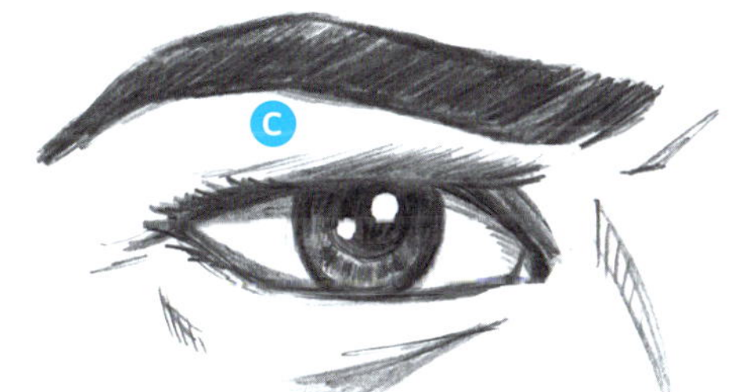


## THE EYES - MALE

A) The upper eyelid is fairly horizontal.
B) The lower eyelid dips.
C) A shine adds life.

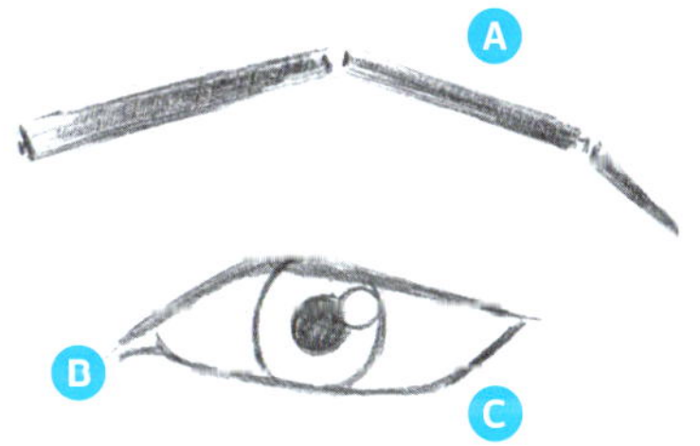


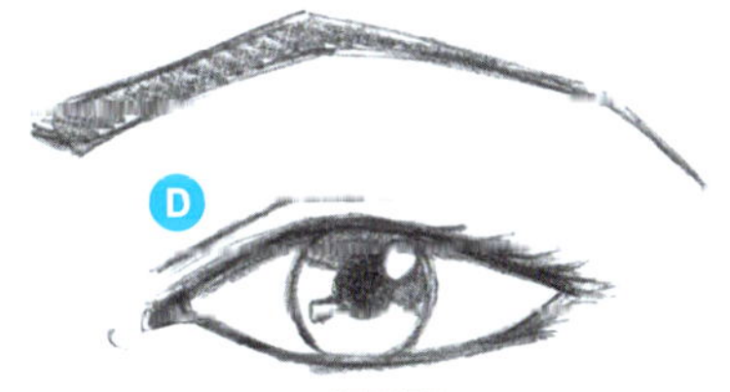


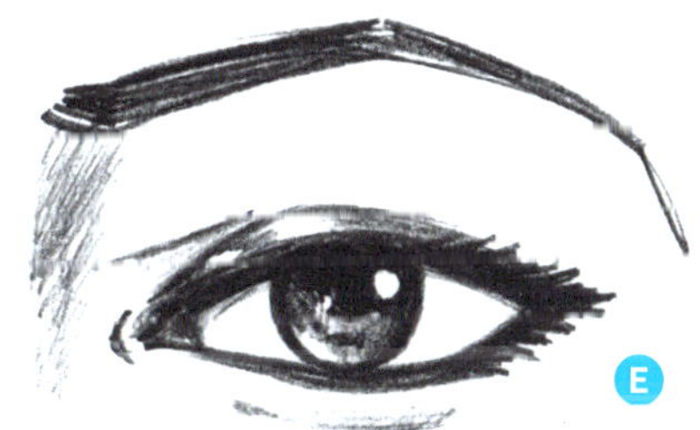


## THE EYES - FEMALE

A) The eyebrow can be broken down Into three smaller lines.
B) Tear duct
C) Dip
D) Eyelid crease
E) The eyelids are darkened, and feathered at the ends.

# THE NOSE

Here's a helpful tip for drawing the nose. The Center Line (that blue guideline you see running down the bridge of the nose) is a great tool for drawing the nose in the correct proportions. Using the Center Line as your landmark, make sure that the left nostril is the same distance from the Center Line as the right nostril. That way, the nose will always look symmetrical.

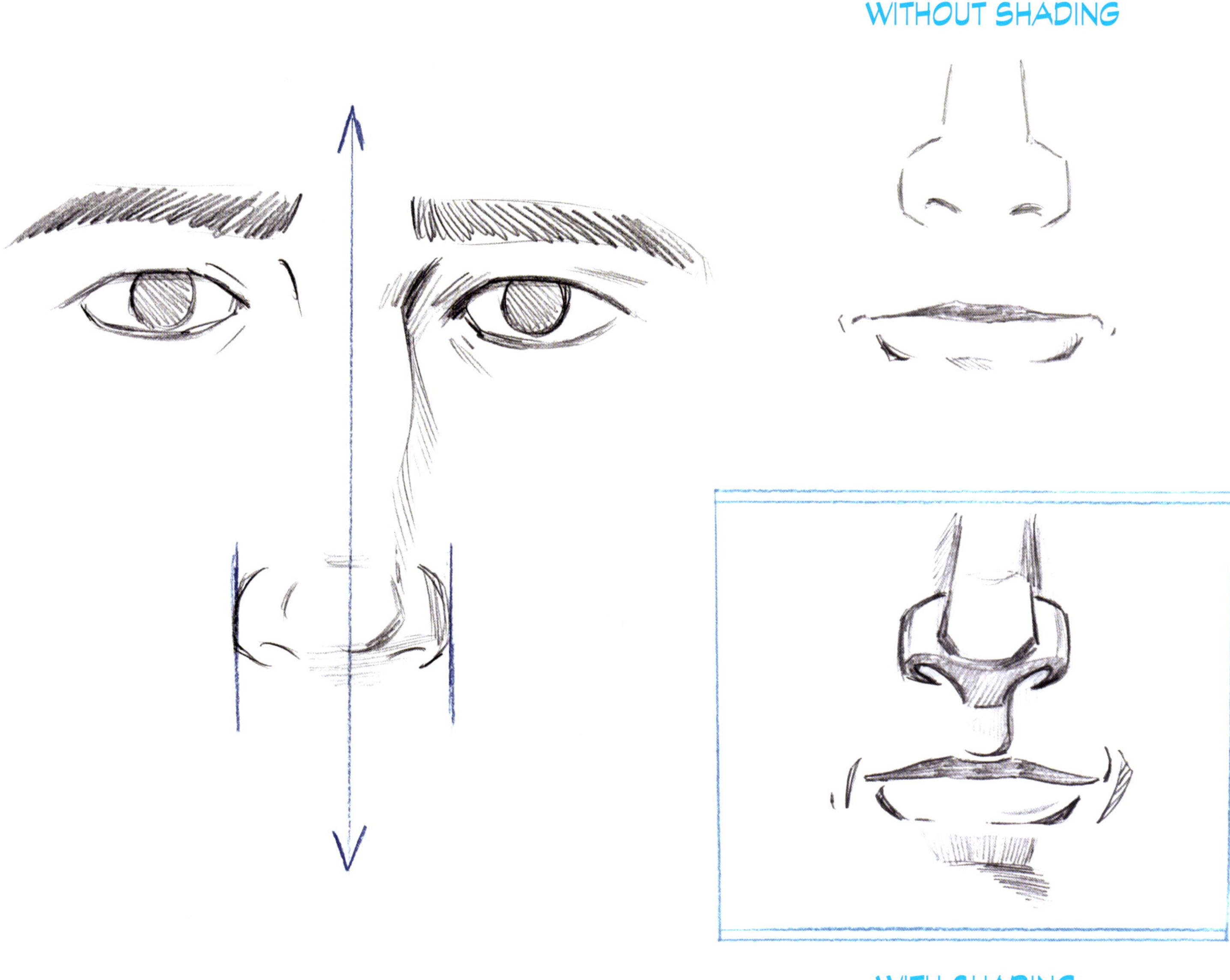

# NOTES ON THE SUBTLE NOSE

When drawing a less pronounced nose, use only a sparing amount of shadow to indicate the side planes of the bridge of the nose, and add a touch of shadow to the underside.

Shading can add glamour to the eyes.

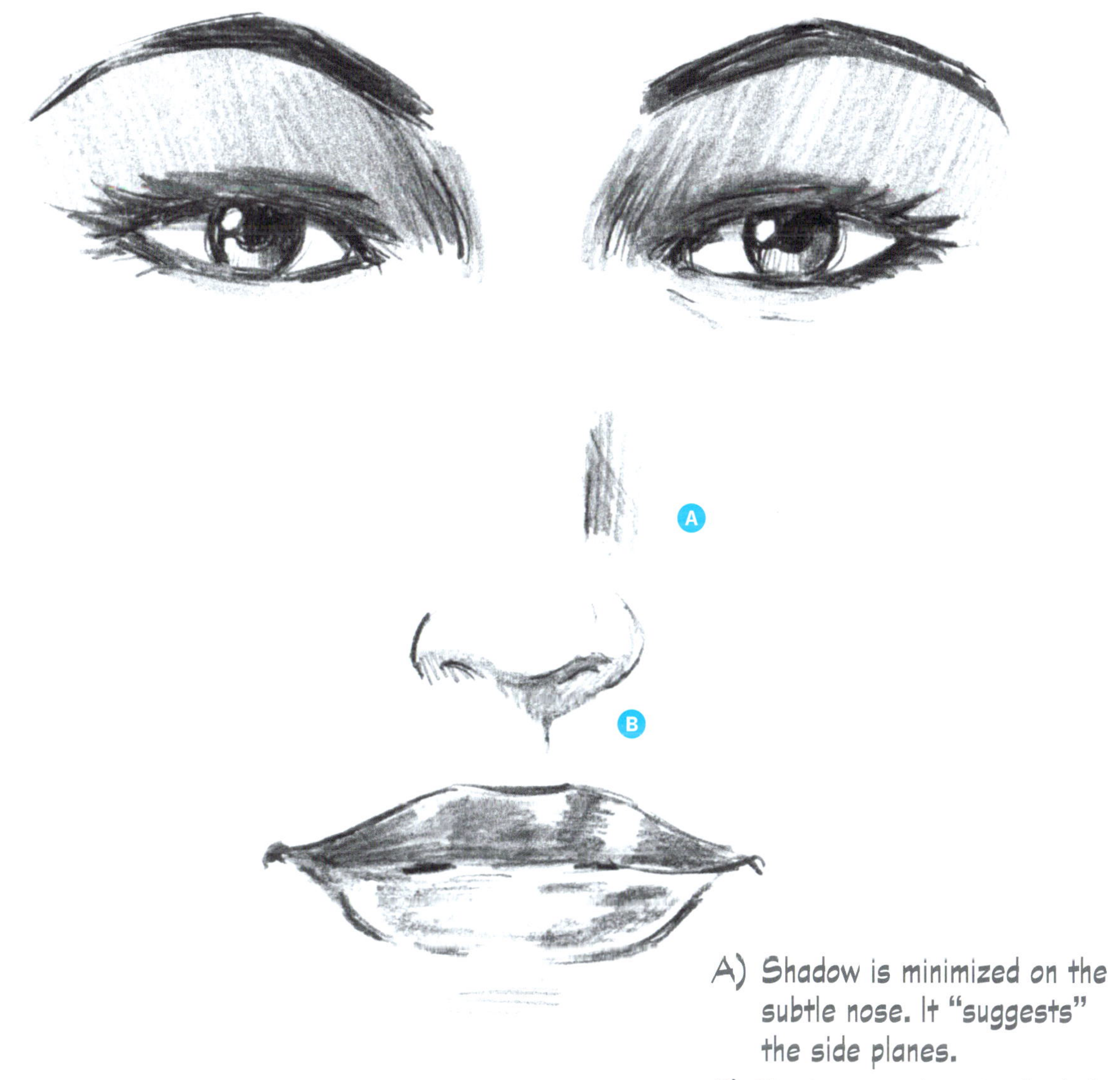


A) Shadow is minimized on the subtle nose. It "suggests" the side planes.

B) The bottom plane is shaded.

# THE LIPS

The difference between the male and female lips is more than the size or "fullness." It also has to do with the overall shape of each.

## ROUGH MALE LIPS

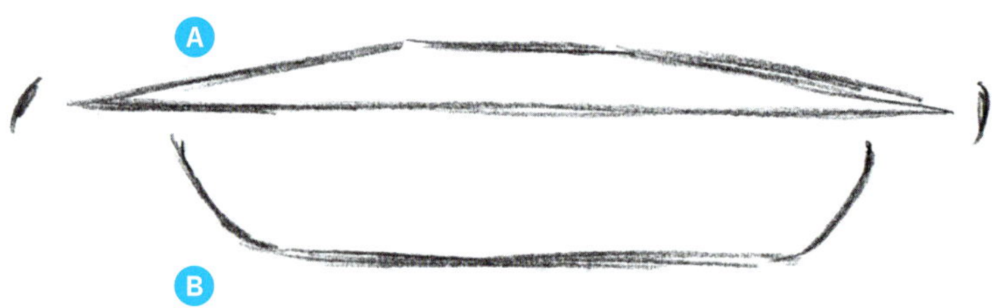


### MALE

A) Thin upper lip, fairly straight across, without much dip in the middle

B) Full lower lip (slightly square), with shadow under the center

## FINISHED MALE LIPS

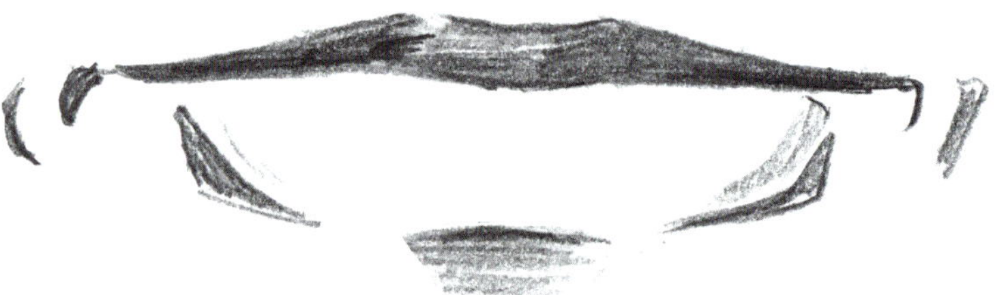

## ROUGH FEMALE LIPS

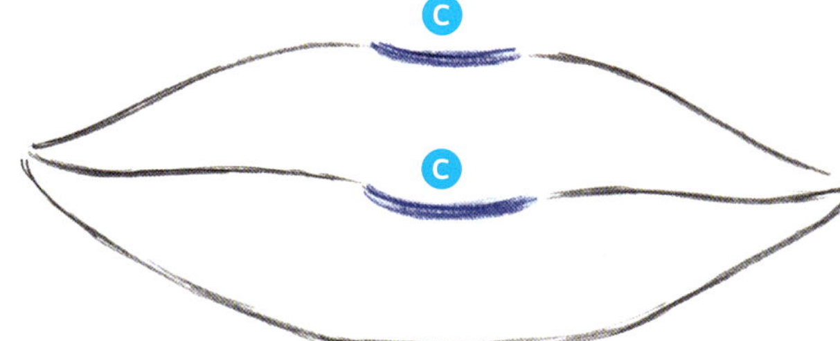


### FEMALE

C) Note the depressions in the upper and lower lips.

D) Thicker lips are bolder, with highlights.

## FINISHED FEMALE LIPS

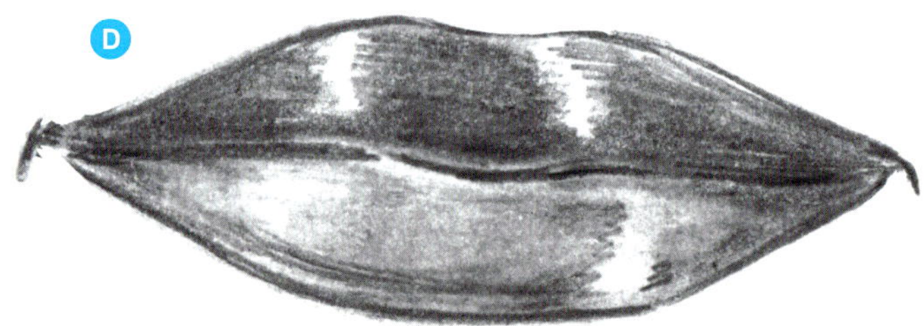

# SHADING

Without shading, a face can appear flat. But with the addition of a few, soft pencil strokes, the image comes to life. Pockets of shadow generally appear in sunken areas, like the orbits of the eyes under the eyebrows. Shadows also appear along side the planes that protrude, such as the nose.

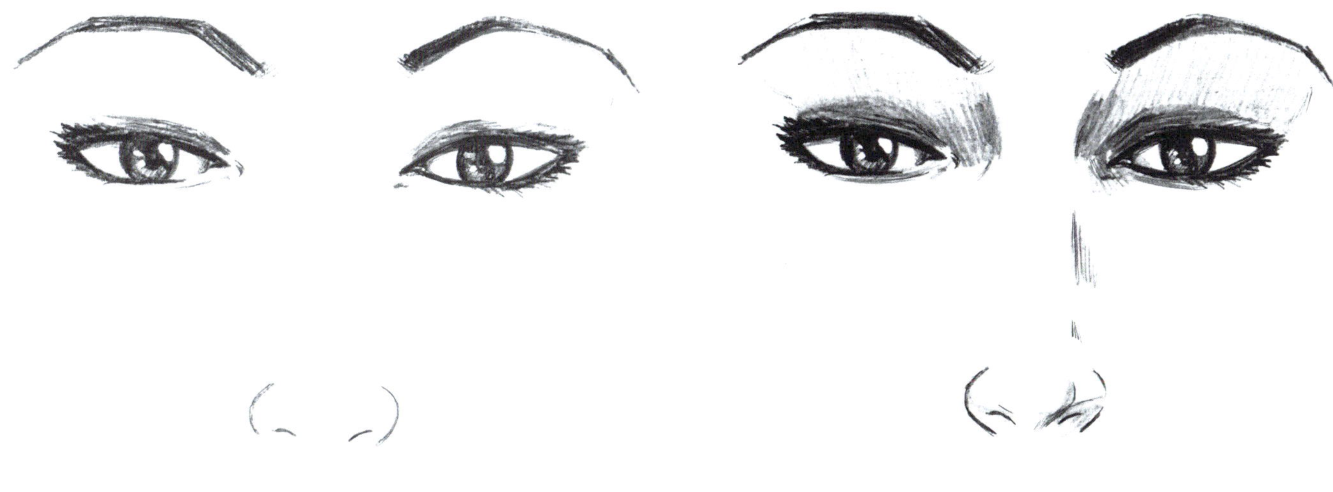

Female Features - Line work only

Female Features - With shading

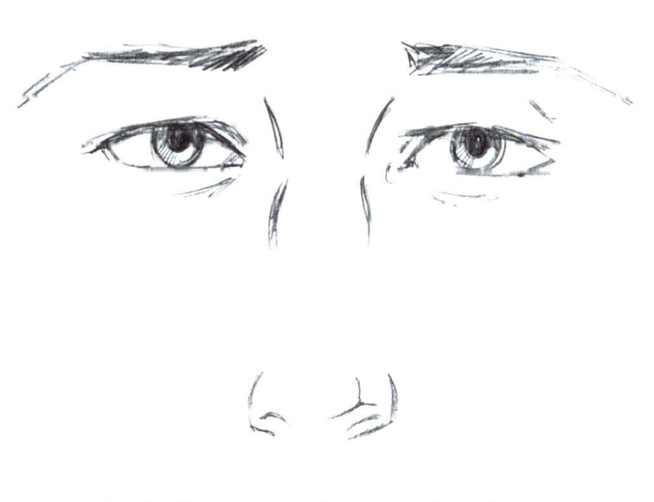

Male Features - Line work only

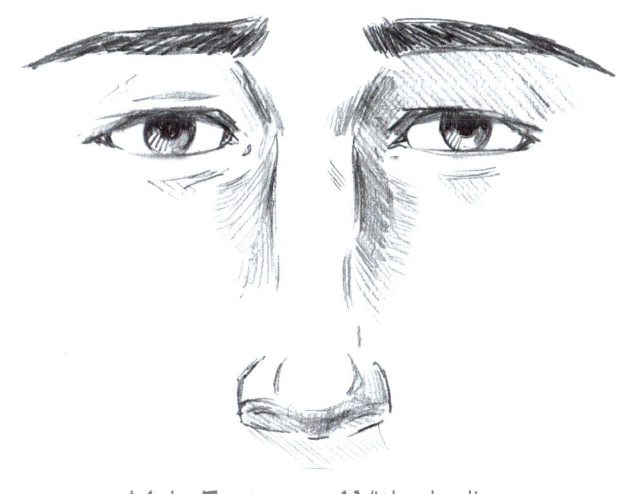

Male Features - With shading

# FEMALE FACE —FRONT VIEW

Now let's create the basic head with what could best be described as an oval that is tapered at the chin. We'll use two basic guidelines to help keep the features in place: the Center Line, which travels up and down, and the Eye Line, which travels side to side.

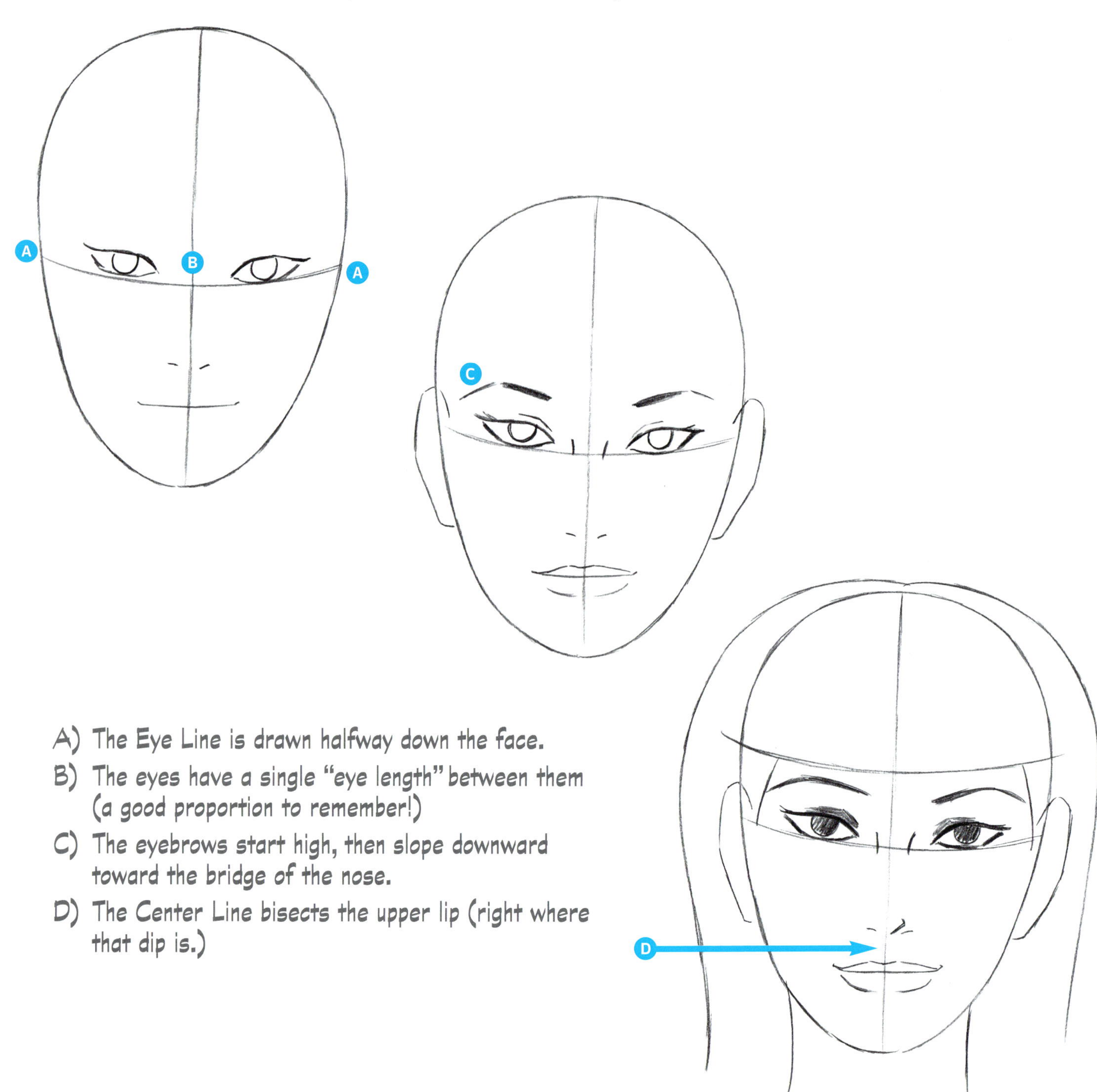


A) The Eye Line is drawn halfway down the face.
B) The eyes have a single "eye length" between them (a good proportion to remember!)
C) The eyebrows start high, then slope downward toward the bridge of the nose.
D) The Center Line bisects the upper lip (right where that dip is.)

# HOW THE EYE LINE HELPS

By utilizing the Eye Line as a guide, you end up with a face that looks symmetrical and correct. Notice that both eyes are on the same level. One isn't slightly higher than the other. We can take this principle one step further: the eyebrows are drawn at the same height as well. Likewise, the top and bottom of the left ear are drawn at the same level as the top and bottom of the right ear.

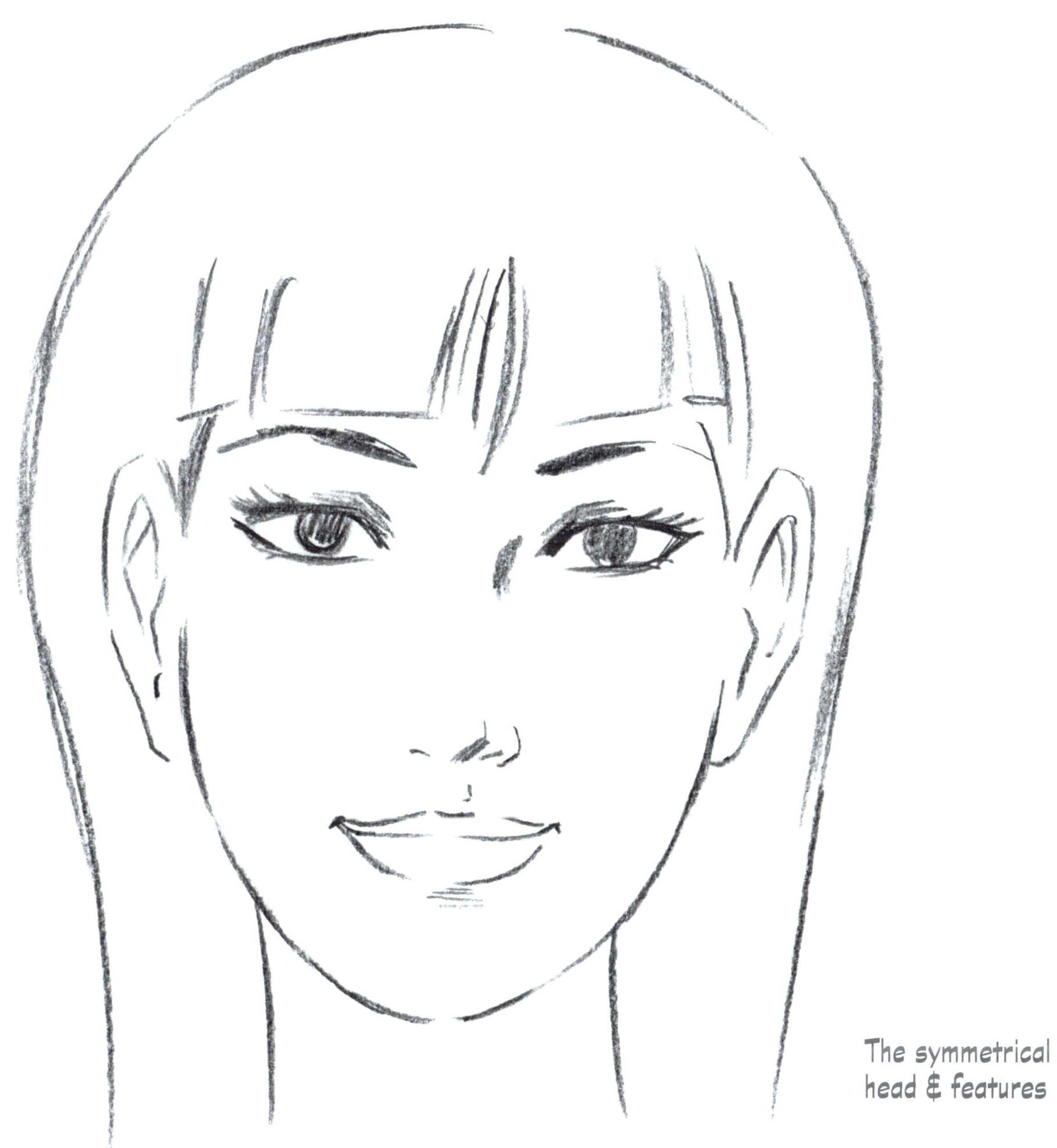

The symmetrical head & features

# MALE FACE—FRONT VIEW

Typically, small adjustments are made to the overall structure of the head in order to create the male face. The jawline and chin are wider and more angular. The neck also appears wider and straighter.

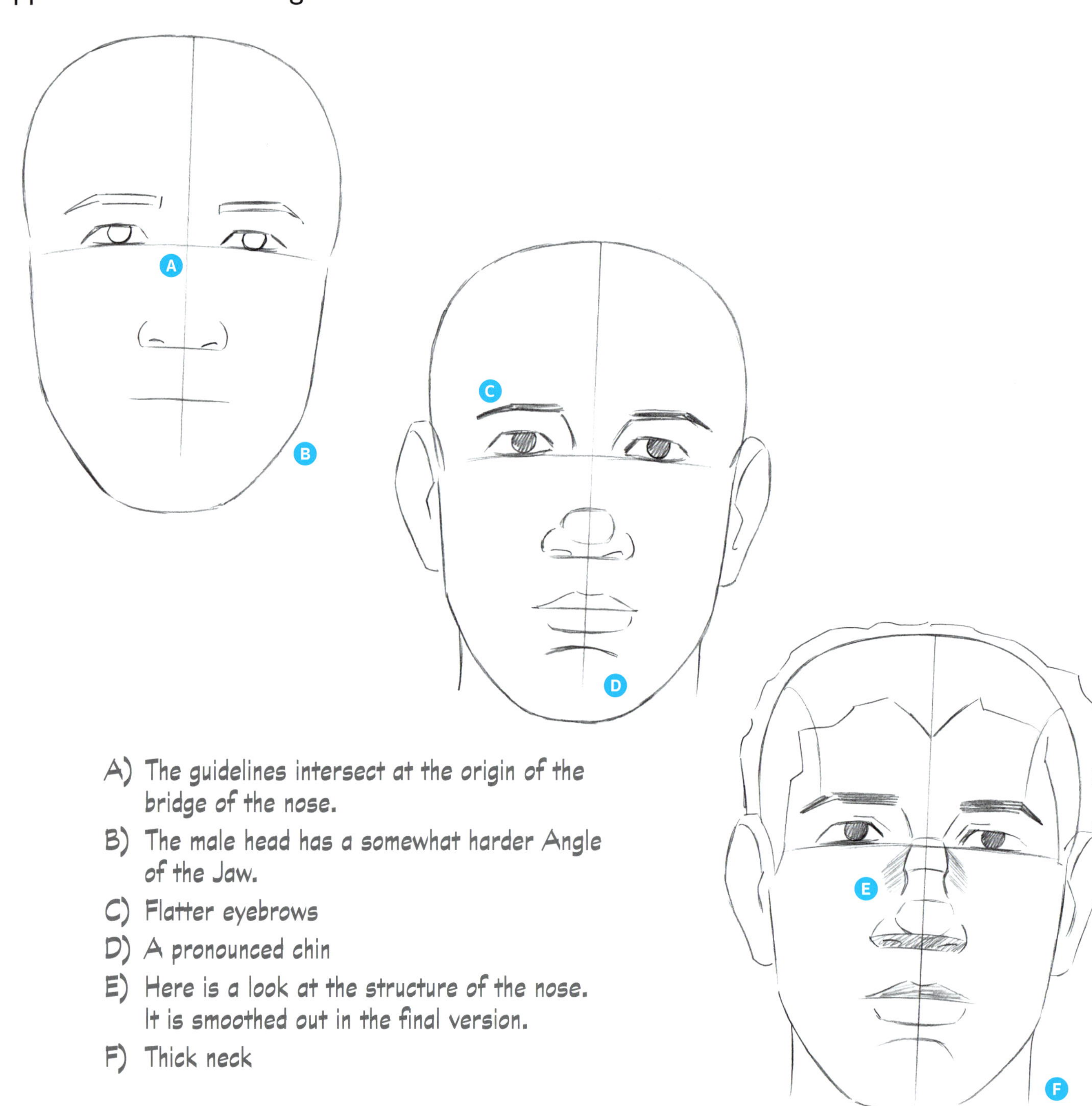


A) The guidelines intersect at the origin of the bridge of the nose.

B) The male head has a somewhat harder Angle of the Jaw.

C) Flatter eyebrows

D) A pronounced chin

E) Here is a look at the structure of the nose. It is smoothed out in the final version.

F) Thick neck

# HOW THE CENTER LINE HELPS

The Center Line is used as an invisible guide to keep the features centered on the face. For example, both eyebrows are equidistant from the Center Line. The nose is centered along it, and the nostrils are equidistant from it. The lips are bisected by it. Note the dip in the middle of the hairline. This is the lowest point of the hairline on the forehead and it is also positioned on the Center Line.

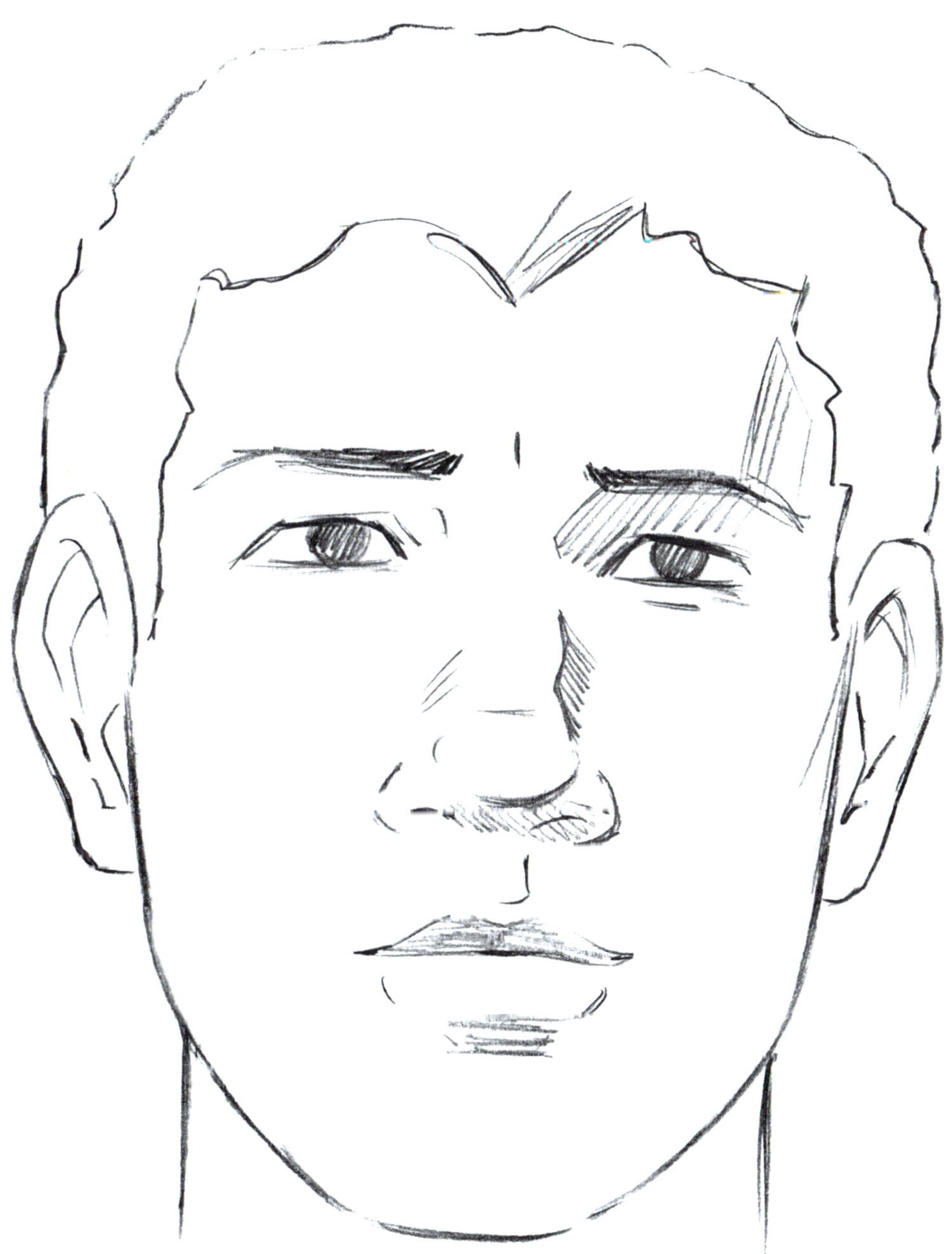

# FEMALE FACE—SIDE VIEW

Hair can cover a good bit of the outline of the head. But don't skip the basic construction phase. Draw a solid head structure at the outset, even if you won't see much of it in the final drawing. It will result in a more effective image.

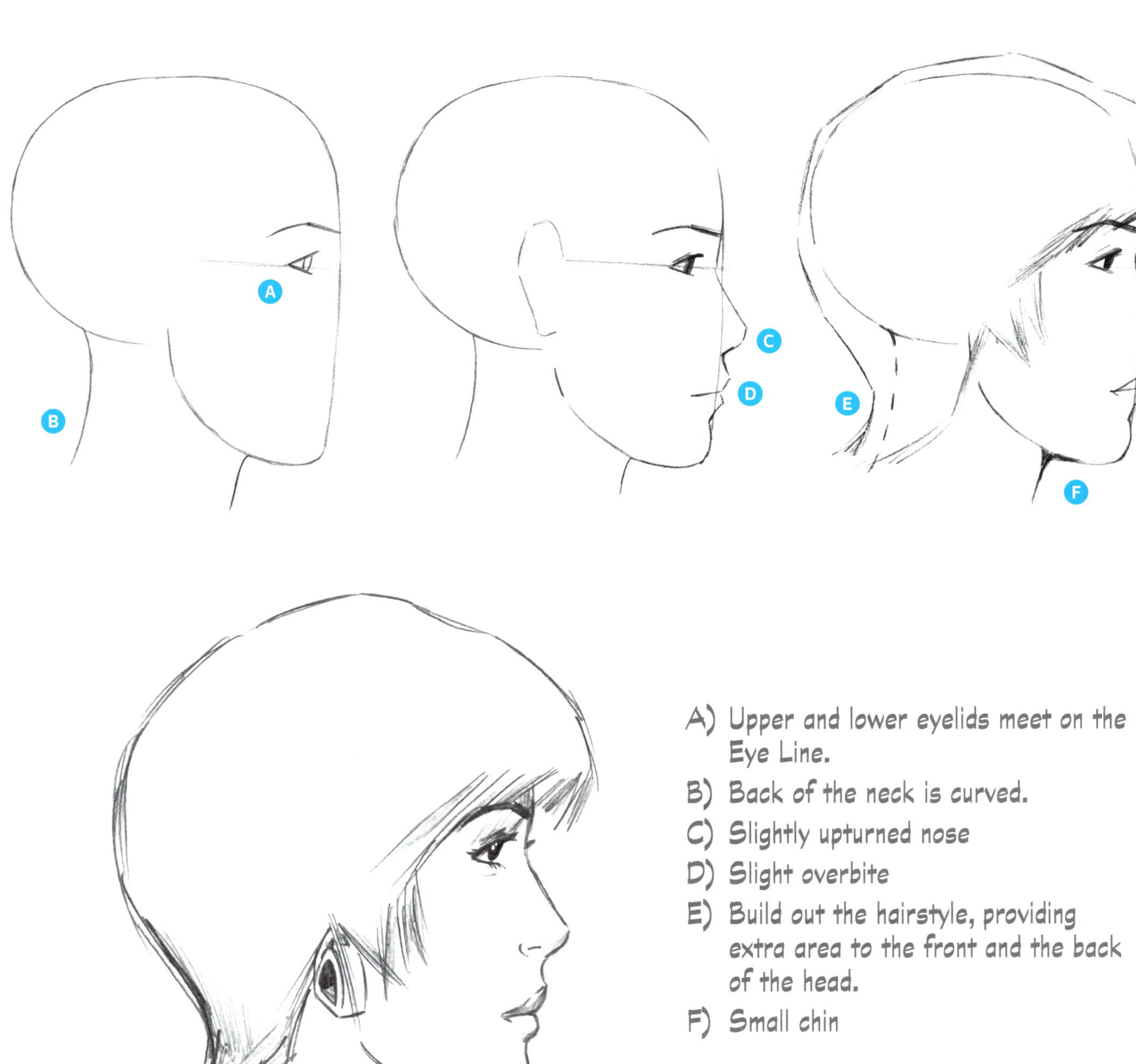


A) Upper and lower eyelids meet on the Eye Line.
B) Back of the neck is curved.
C) Slightly upturned nose
D) Slight overbite
E) Build out the hairstyle, providing extra area to the front and the back of the head.
F) Small chin

# MALE FACE —SIDE VIEW

The tip of the nose is the most prominent part of the face in profile. Don't be shy about drawing a bold, diagonal line to establish its position.

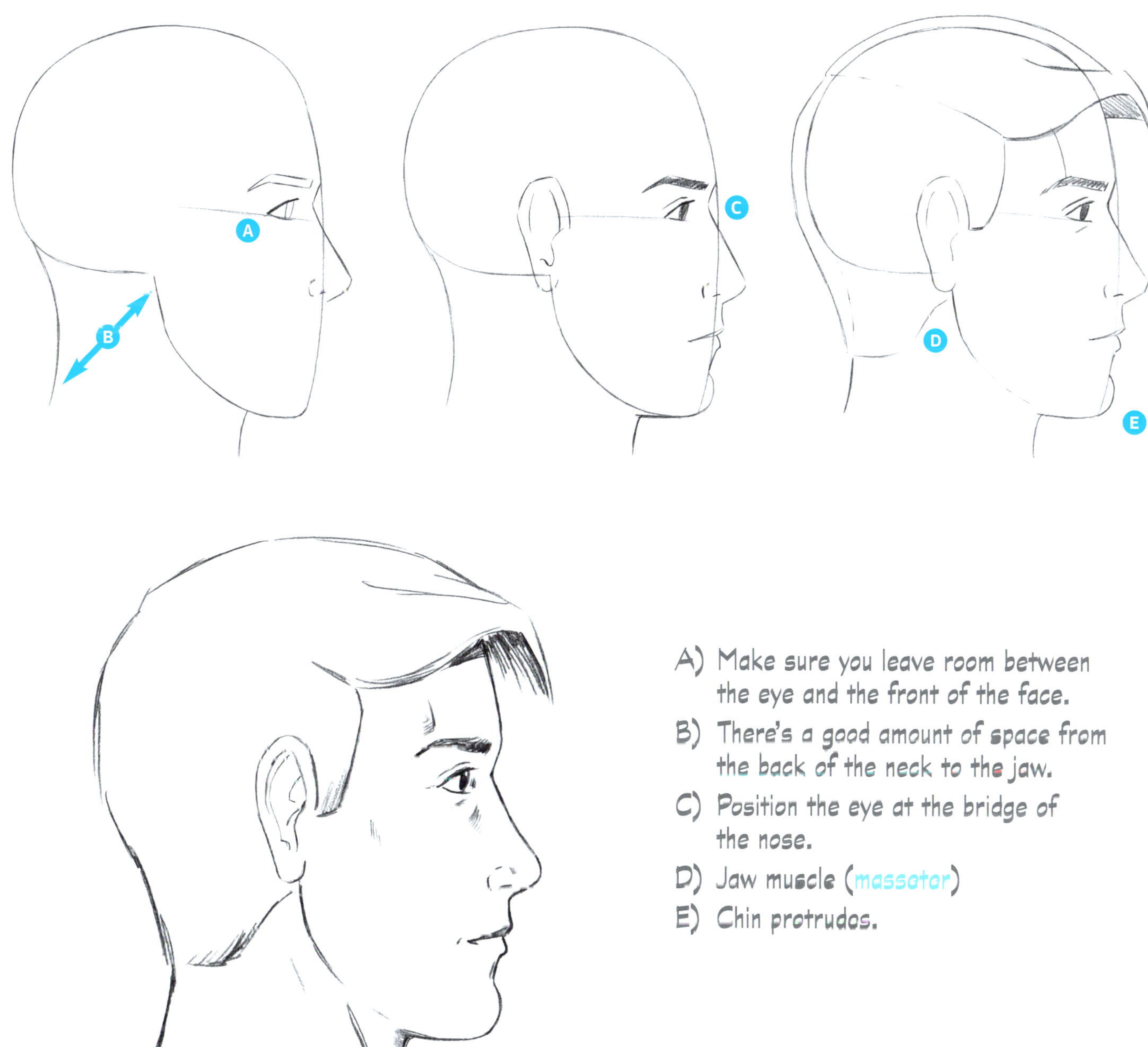


A) Make sure you leave room between the eye and the front of the face.

B) There's a good amount of space from the back of the neck to the jaw.

C) Position the eye at the bridge of the nose.

D) Jaw muscle (masseter)

E) Chin protrudes.

# DRAWING THE BODY: BASIC SECTIONS

In the same way that we simplified the head in the first section, we will also simplify the body, which makes it easier to conceptualize and draw the human figure. Let's start with the torso, which is the pillar of the human figure.

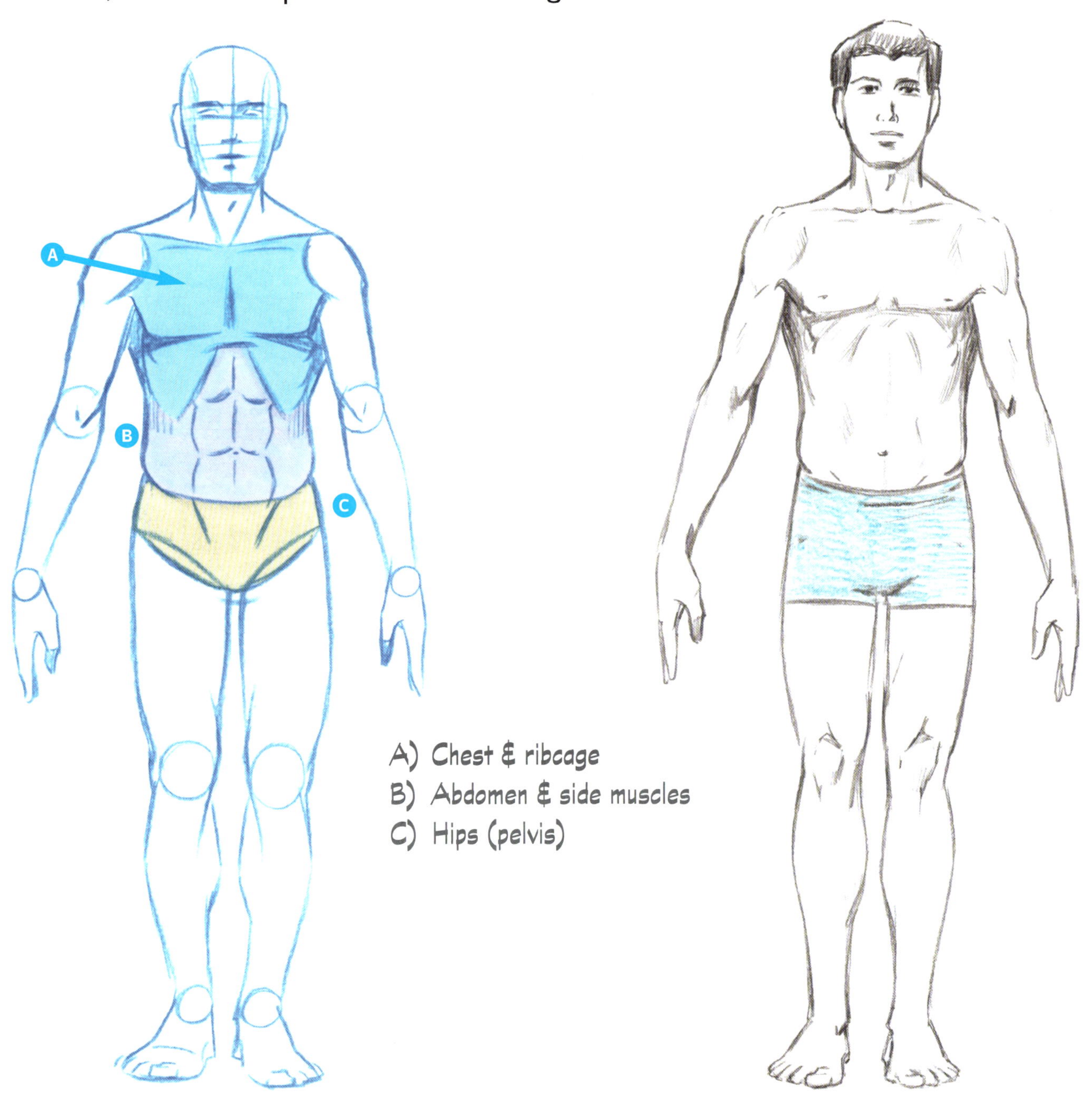

# FEMALE—UPPER BODY

Because female figures have high waistlines, we can attach the midsection to the upper torso, leaving us with just two basic shapes: upper and lower.

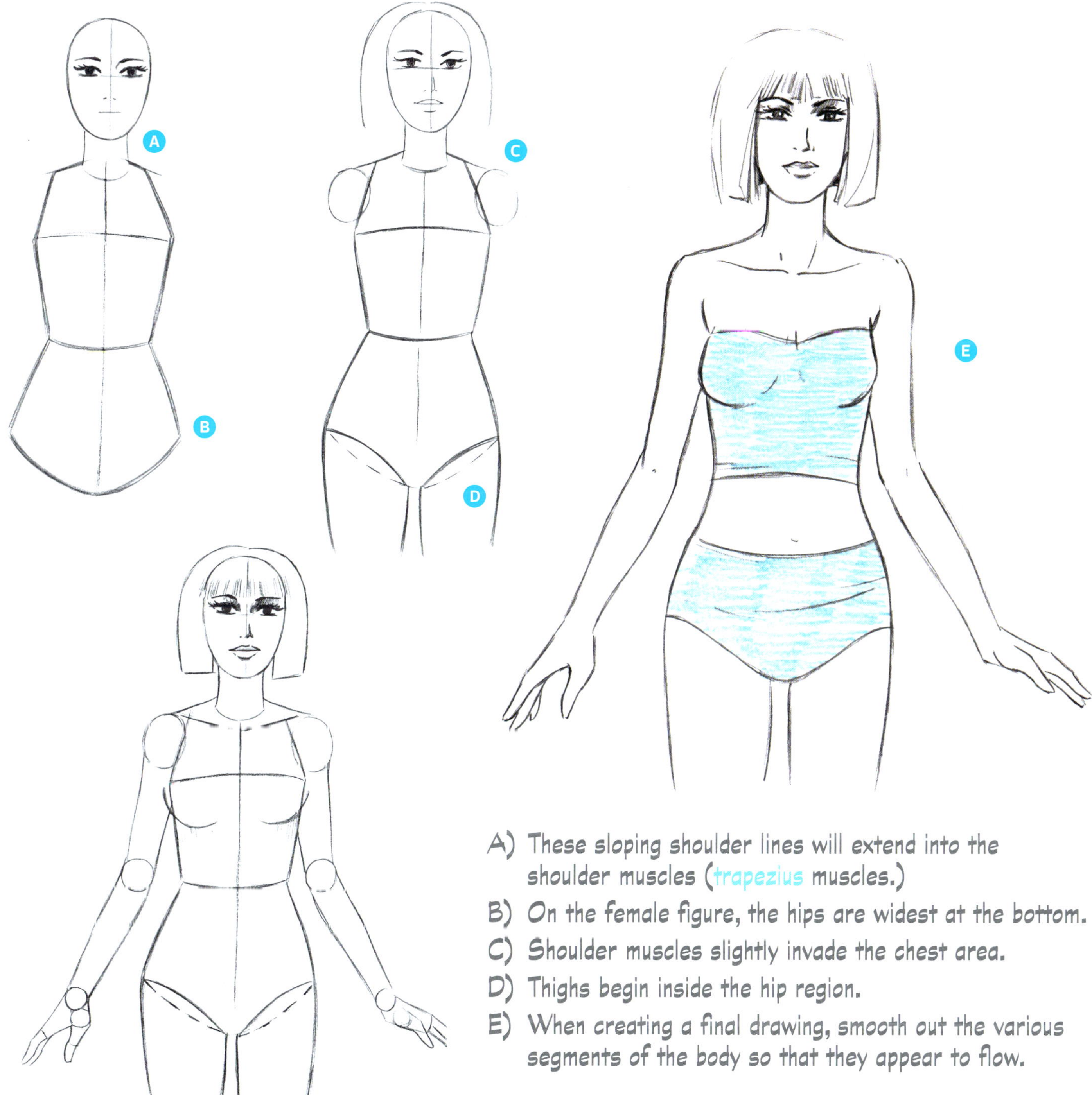


A) These sloping shoulder lines will extend into the shoulder muscles (trapezius muscles.)

B) On the female figure, the hips are widest at the bottom.

C) Shoulder muscles slightly invade the chest area.

D) Thighs begin inside the hip region.

E) When creating a final drawing, smooth out the various segments of the body so that they appear to flow.

# MALE—UPPER BODY

Now let's depart from strictly symmetrical poses. In this drawing, the arms are in different positions. In addition, the torso itself is slightly shorter on the left side, and slightly longer on the right side. This dynamic is typical when a person puts more weight on one foot than on the other. In this case, the weight falls on his right leg (his right).

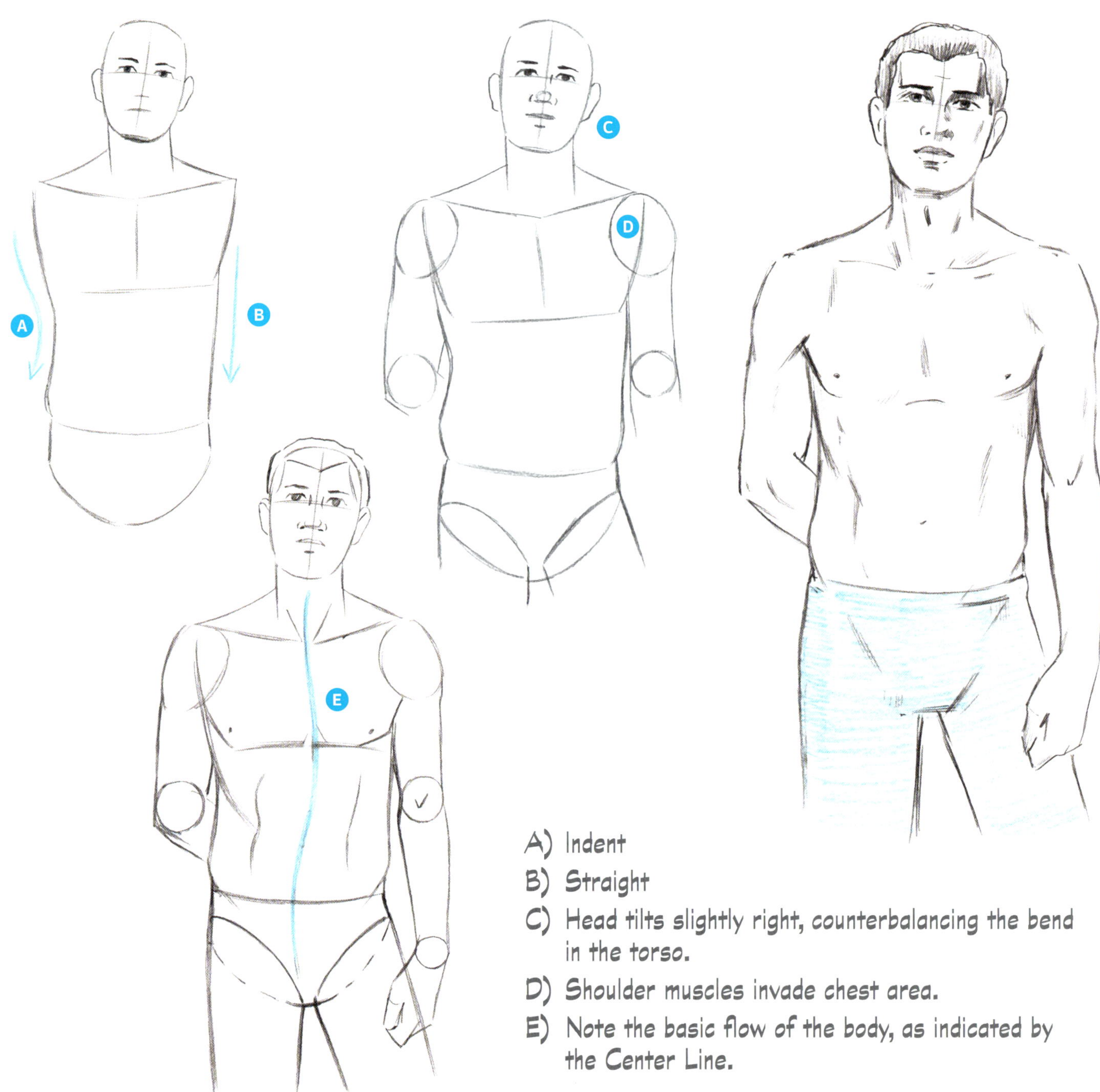


A) Indent
B) Straight
C) Head tilts slightly right, counterbalancing the bend in the torso.
D) Shoulder muscles invade chest area.
E) Note the basic flow of the body, as indicated by the Center Line.

# FLOW OF THE LEGS

Before we begin to draw full-body poses, let's pause to check the basic "flow lines" of the legs. By incorporating the concept of these directional lines, your poses will immediately look more natural.

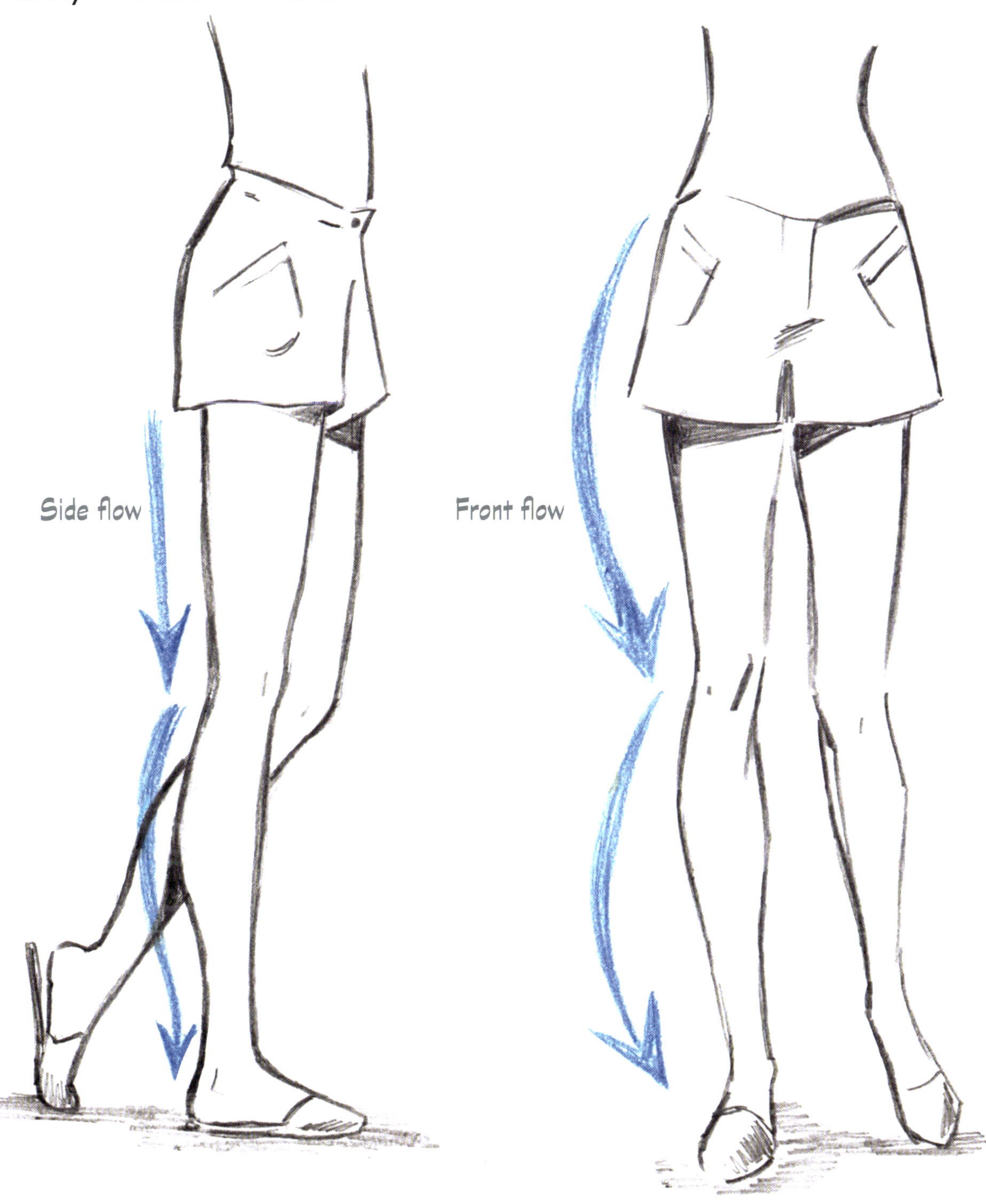

# A NOTE ON HANDS

Don't shy away from drawing hands, even it they are, at first, somewhat challenging. It's really like learning to ride a bicycle—the first few starts are bumpy, but then it starts to become instinctive. And that's because you'll notice similar themes in any hand pose: the joint configuration of the thumb, the various lengths of the fingers, the width of the palm, and so forth.

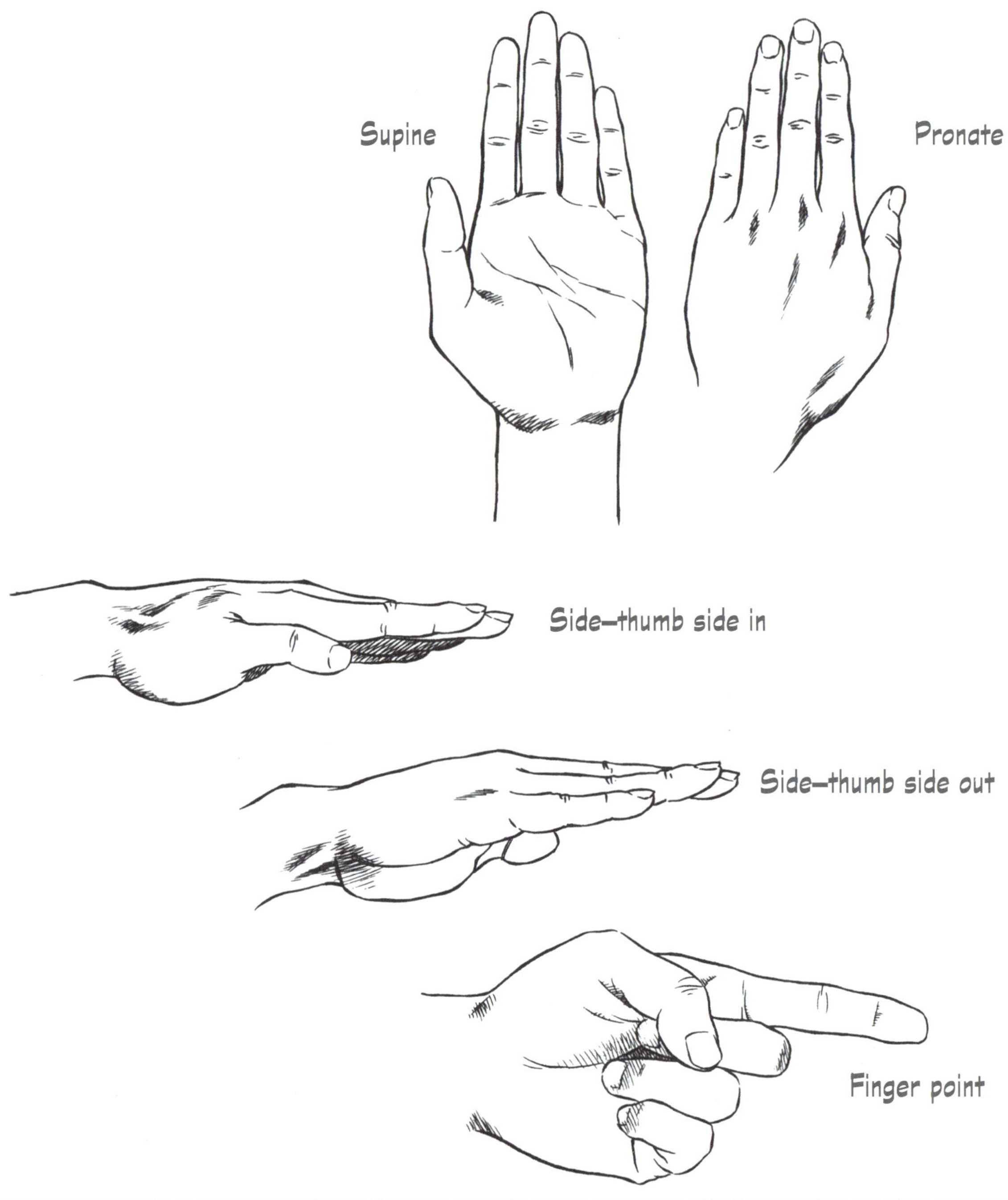

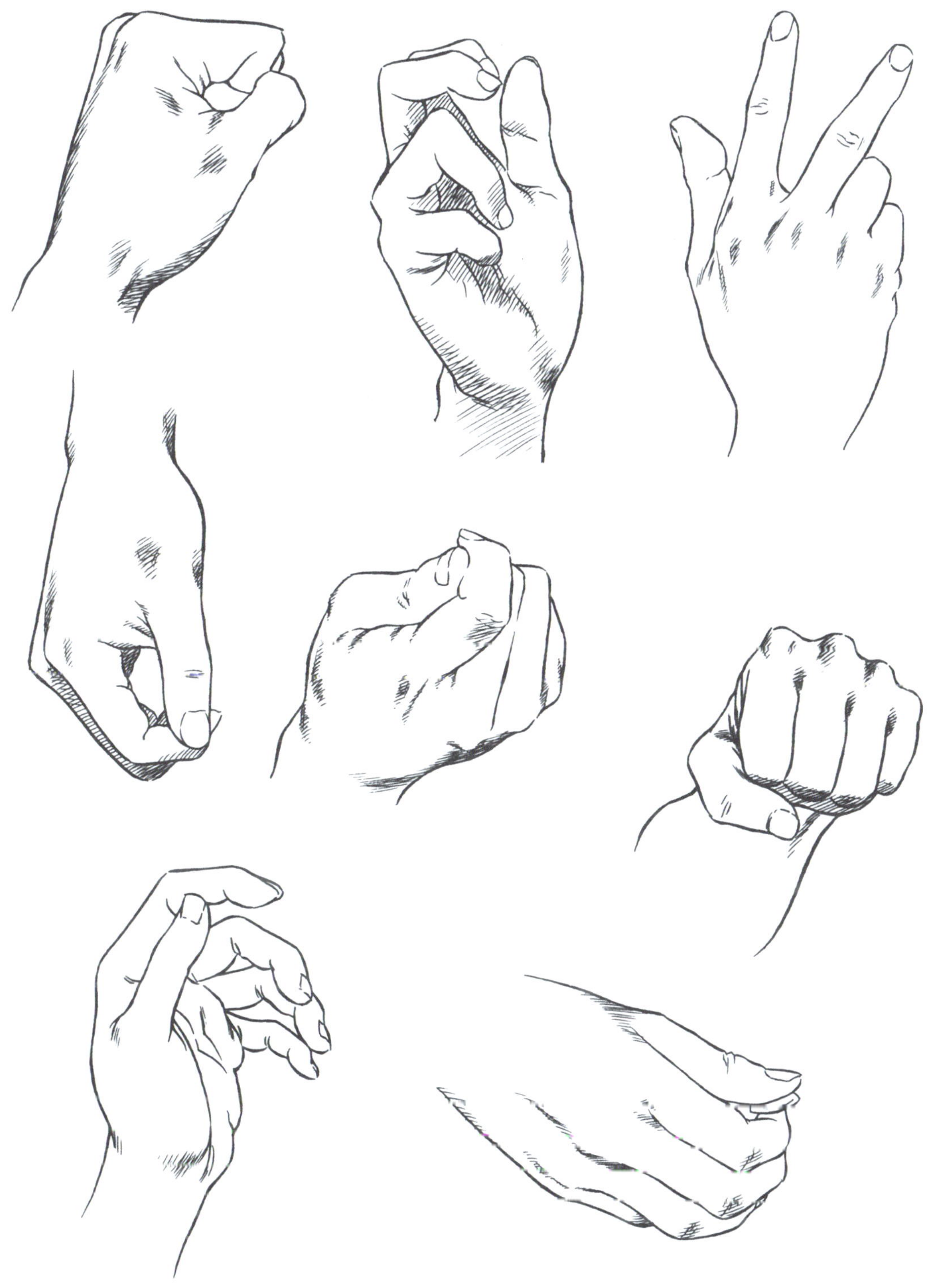

Try making some rough sketches of these examples. Don't look for perfection. You can clean up your drawings as you get more comfortable with the material. There's a lot of reference material here but there's no need to tackle every hand pose. Whenever you're drawing hands, if you feel a little uncertain, flip back to these pages for reference.

# PUTTING IT ALL TOGETHER: THE FULL FIGURE

In the same way that we simplified the head in the first section, we will also simplify the body to make sense of the human figure. To start, let's begin with the torso, which is the "pillar" of the human figure.

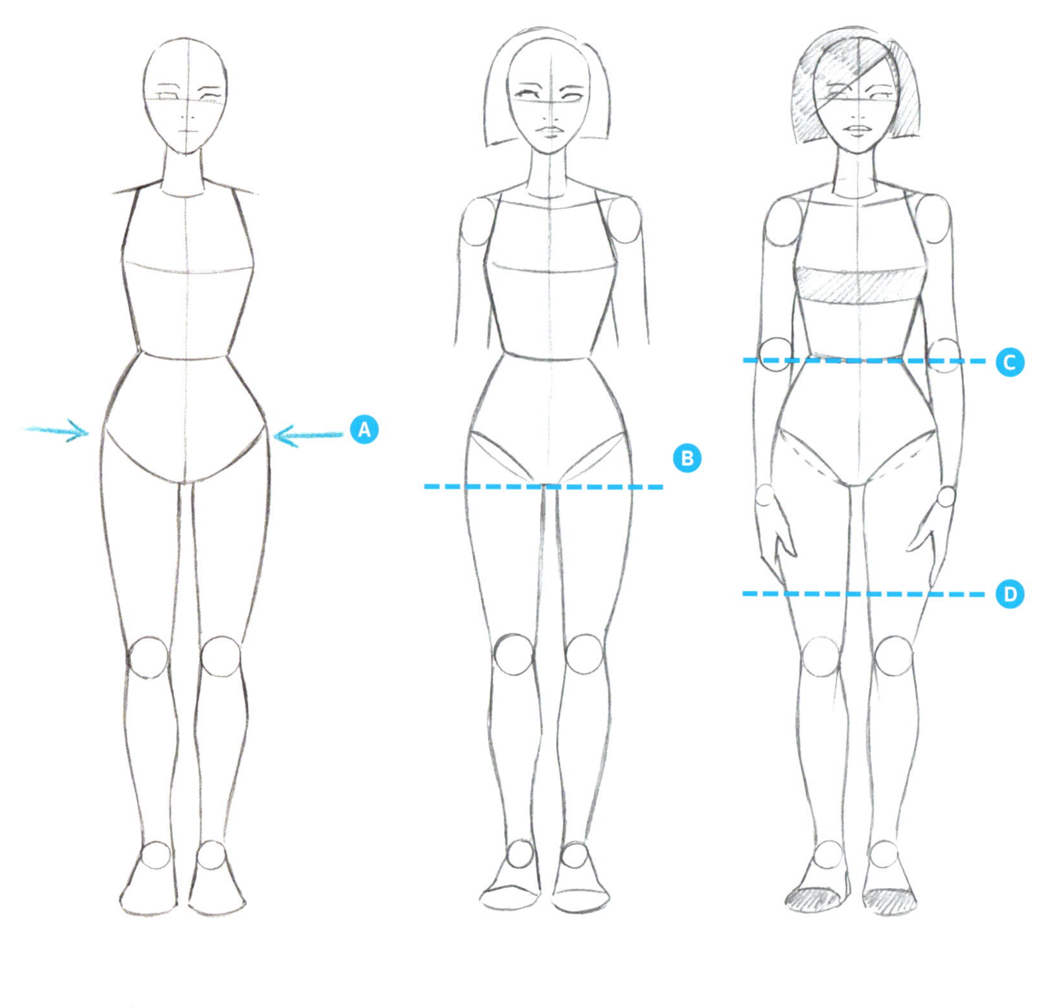


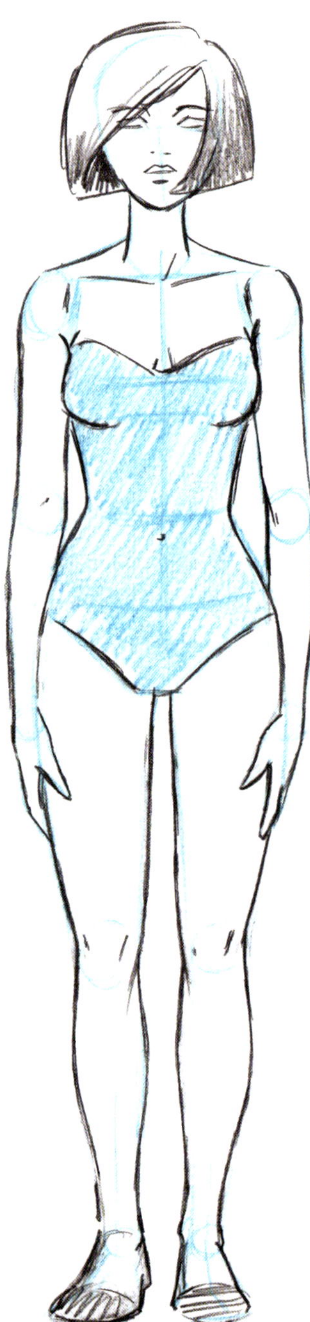

A) Widest point on the female figure
B) Halfway point of the figure, as measured from top to bottom
C) Elbows are drawn where the midsection meets the hips.
D) Hands are midway down the thigh.

# CURVES IN THE SIDE VIEW

The side view is anything but straight and stiff! In fact, when drawn in a natural-looking posture, the side view is one of the most dynamic poses. Although the average viewer doesn't realize it, there's a lot going on in the side view. Here are the techniques you can use to make your side poses come to life.

A) The back is rounded, from the top of the shoulders to the bottom of the shoulder blade.

B) At the bottom of the shoulder blade, the angle of the back makes a deep curve in the lower back.

C) The angle shifts direction again at the hips, sweeping around the buttocks.

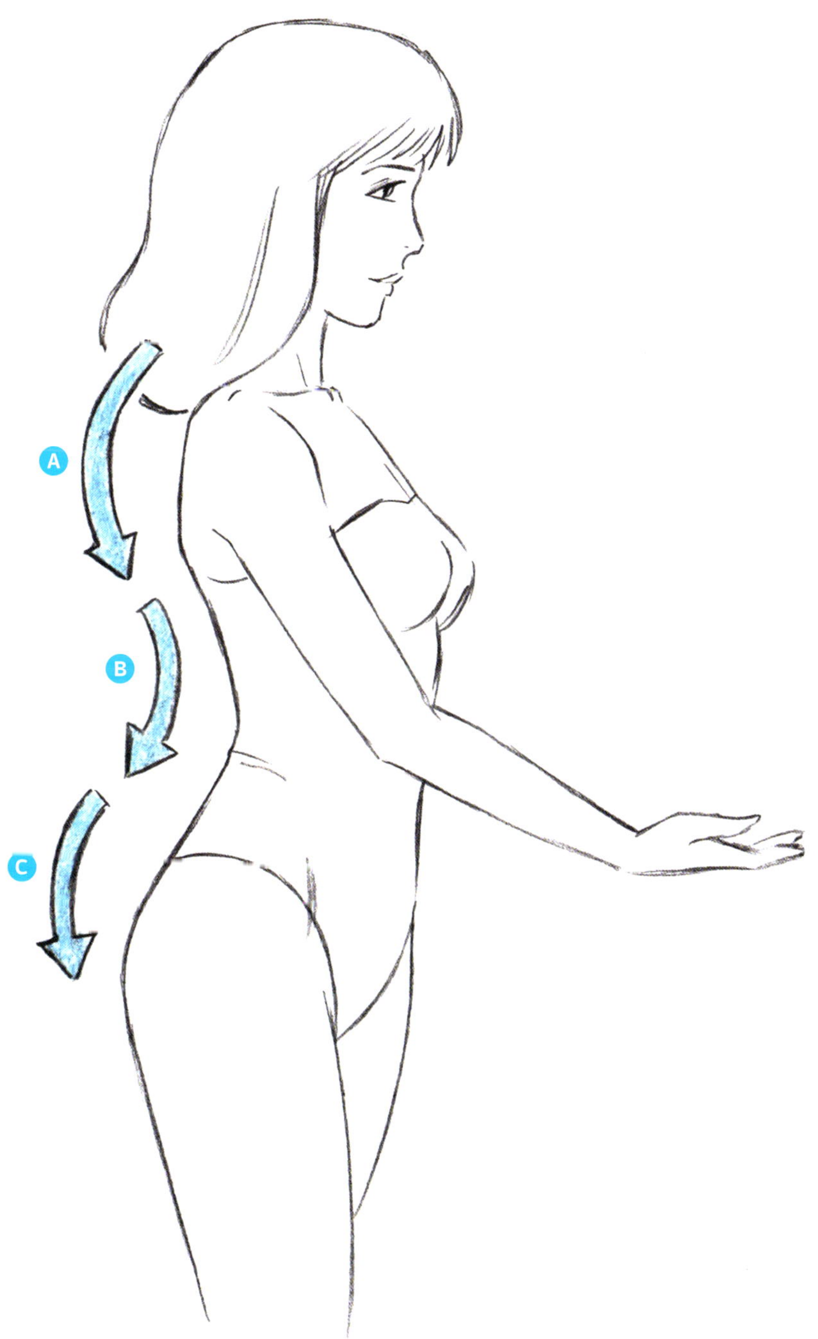

# THE FRONT BODY IN SIDE VIEW

On the previous page, we took note of the natural curves of the back. Now let's look at what happens to the front of the body in the side view. There are still curves, but they are less dramatic, because the front of the torso stretches, which evens it out. This counterbalances the deep curve in the lower back.

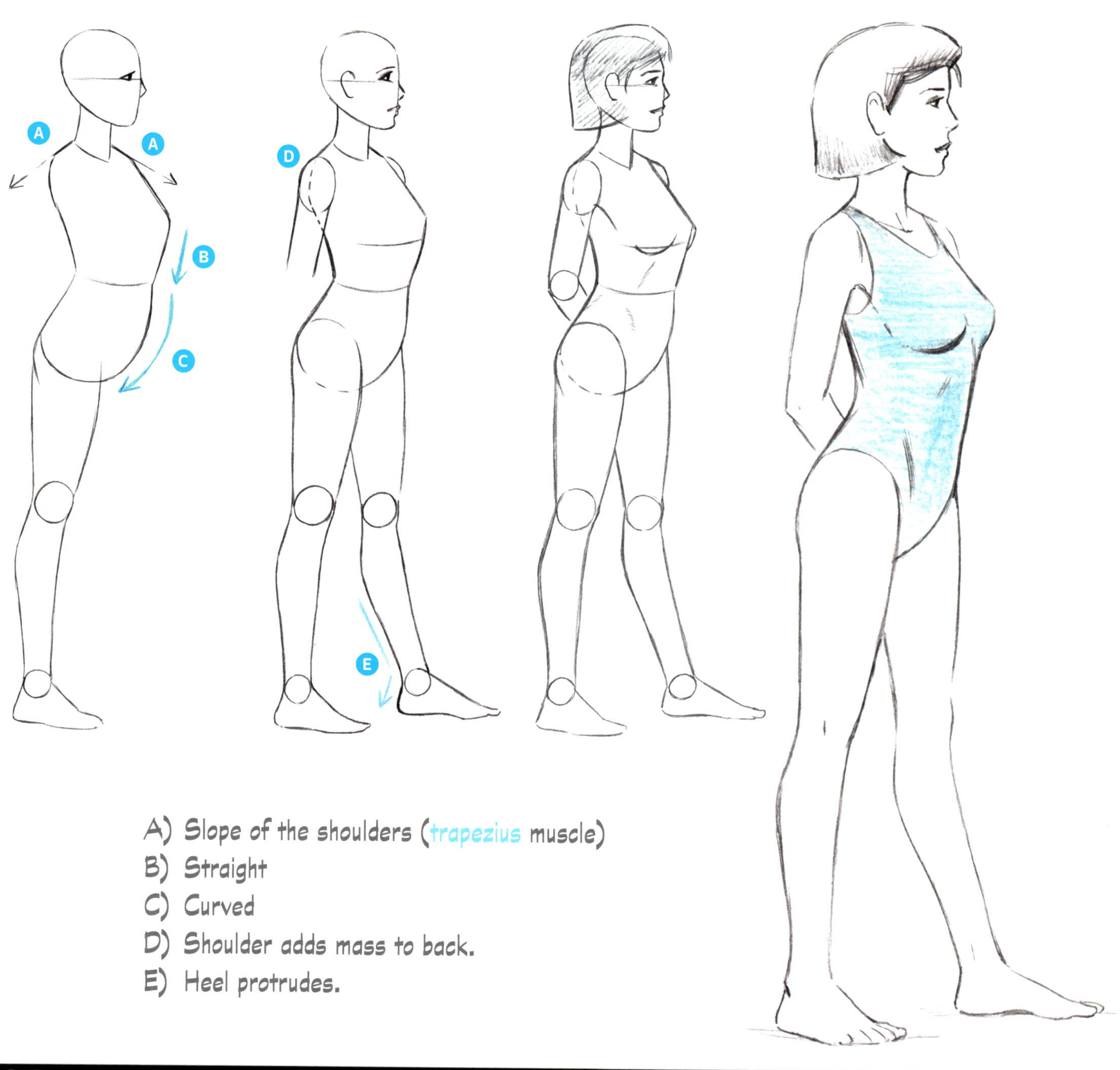


A) Slope of the shoulders (trapezius muscle)
B) Straight
C) Curved
D) Shoulder adds mass to back.
E) Heel protrudes.

# THE RELAXED SIDE VIEW

Casual poses look relaxed and spontaneous—as if you had captured an image of the model off guard. By indicating motion—in this case, the turn of the figure toward us—we create a natural look.

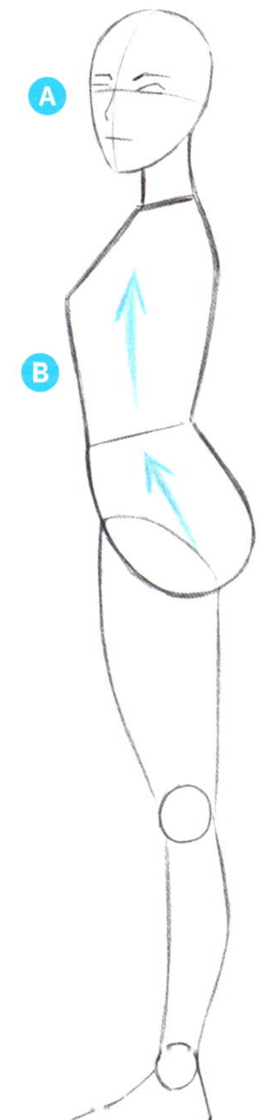


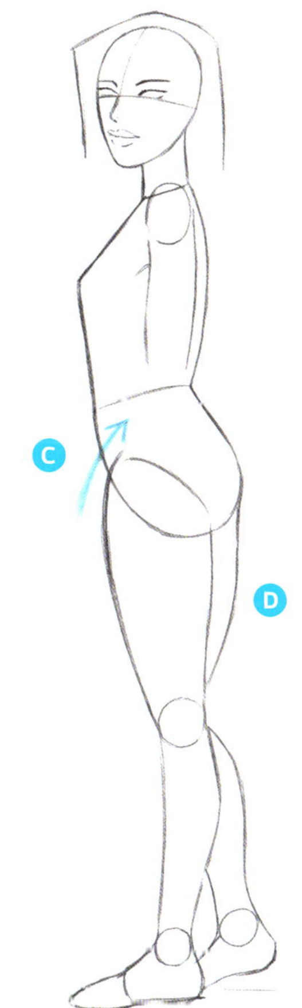


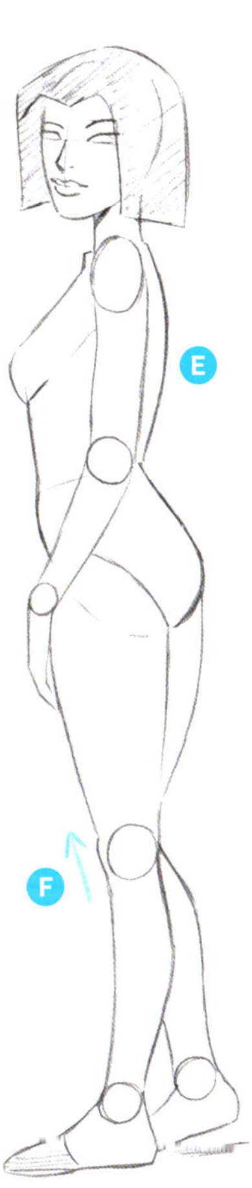


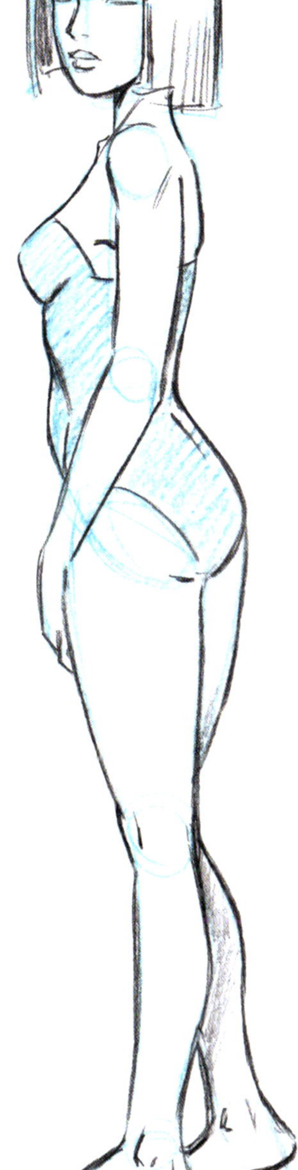

A) Head is in a three-quarter view.
B) Angles of the torso
C) The line of the thigh invades the hip region.
D) The position of the far leg does not mirror the near leg (asymmetrical.)
E) Indicate a portion of the back behind the arm.
F) Knee angles slightly forward; it is not vertical.

# DRAWING THE BACK

What's the first thing you think about when drawing the back? The shoulder blades. And while those are certainly the prominent features of the back, they won't necessarily help you construct it from scratch. Here are some practical pointers that will get you there.

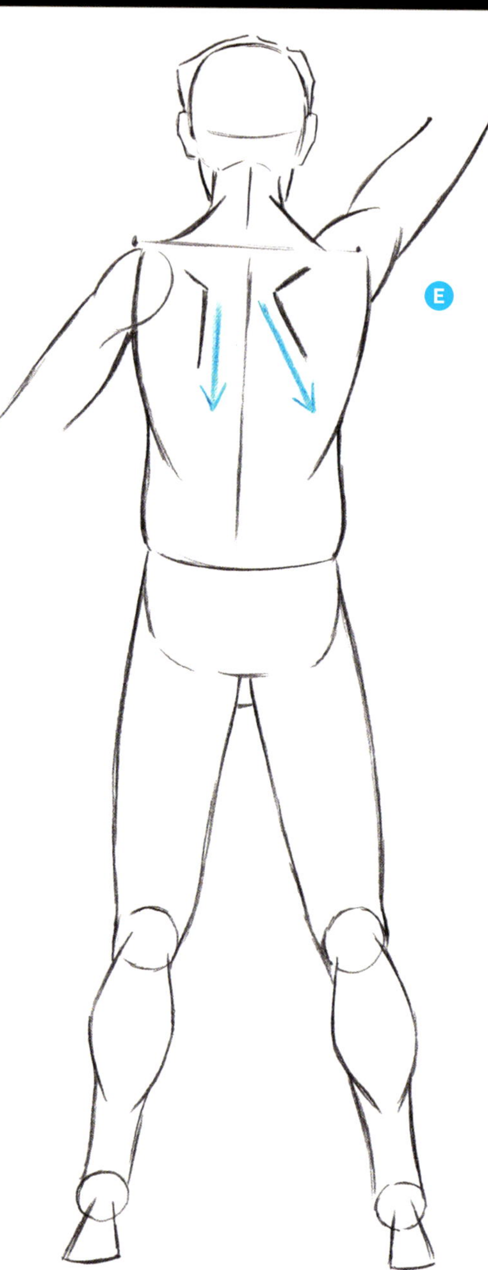


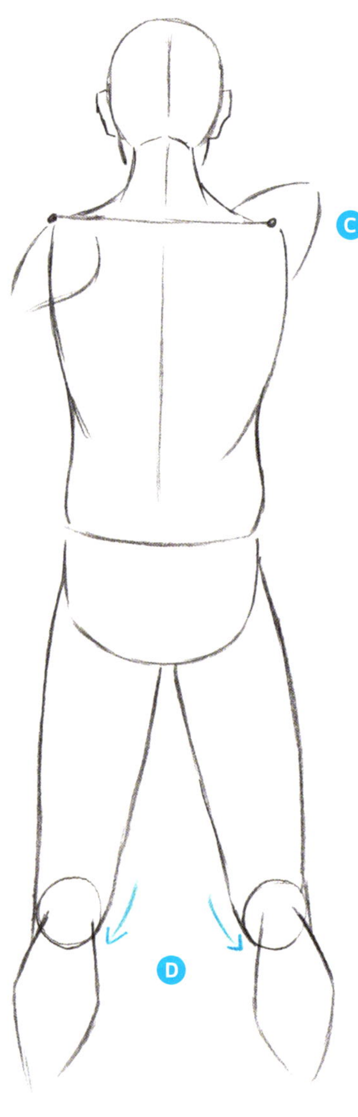


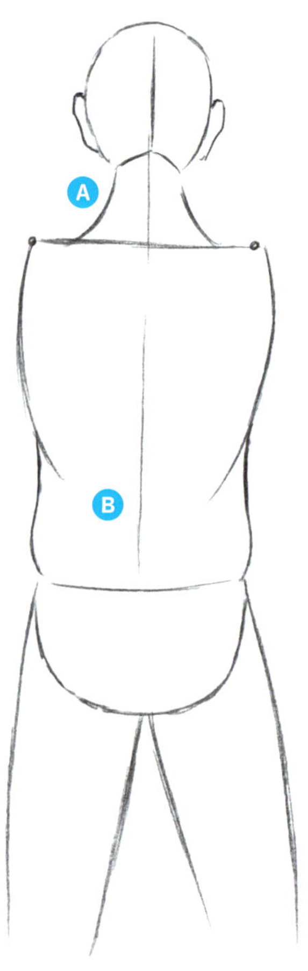


A) The back of neck widens considerably.

B) Indicate the spine, which (conveniently) is also the Center Line!

C) Shoulder muscles taper toward the arms.

D) From the rear, we see that the ligaments of the knees angle inward.

E) The angle of the shoulder blades is pushed or pulled in different directions by the positions of the arms.

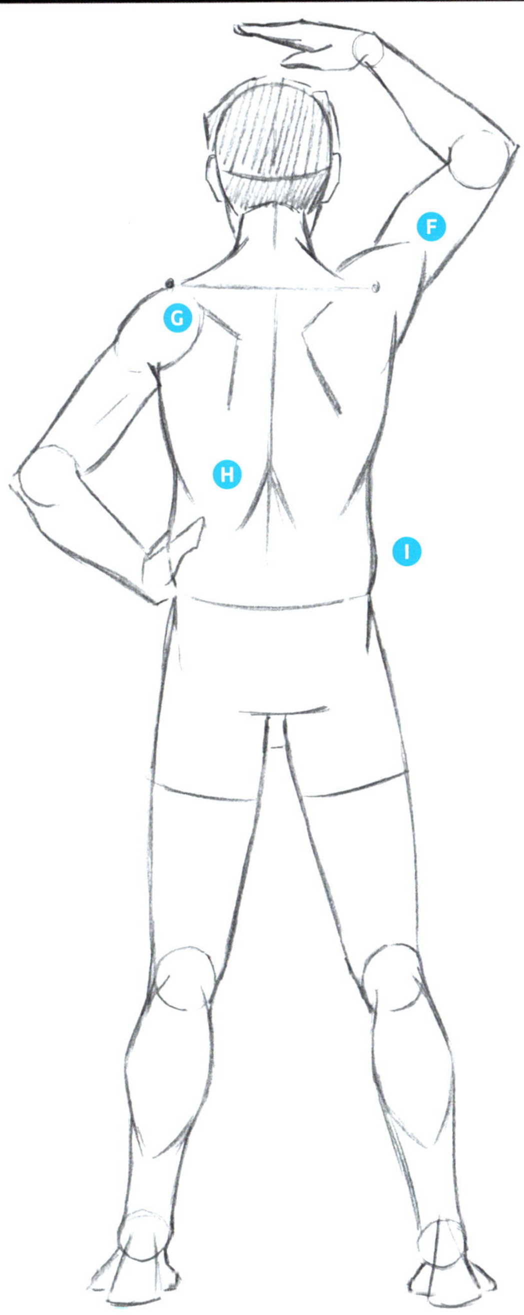

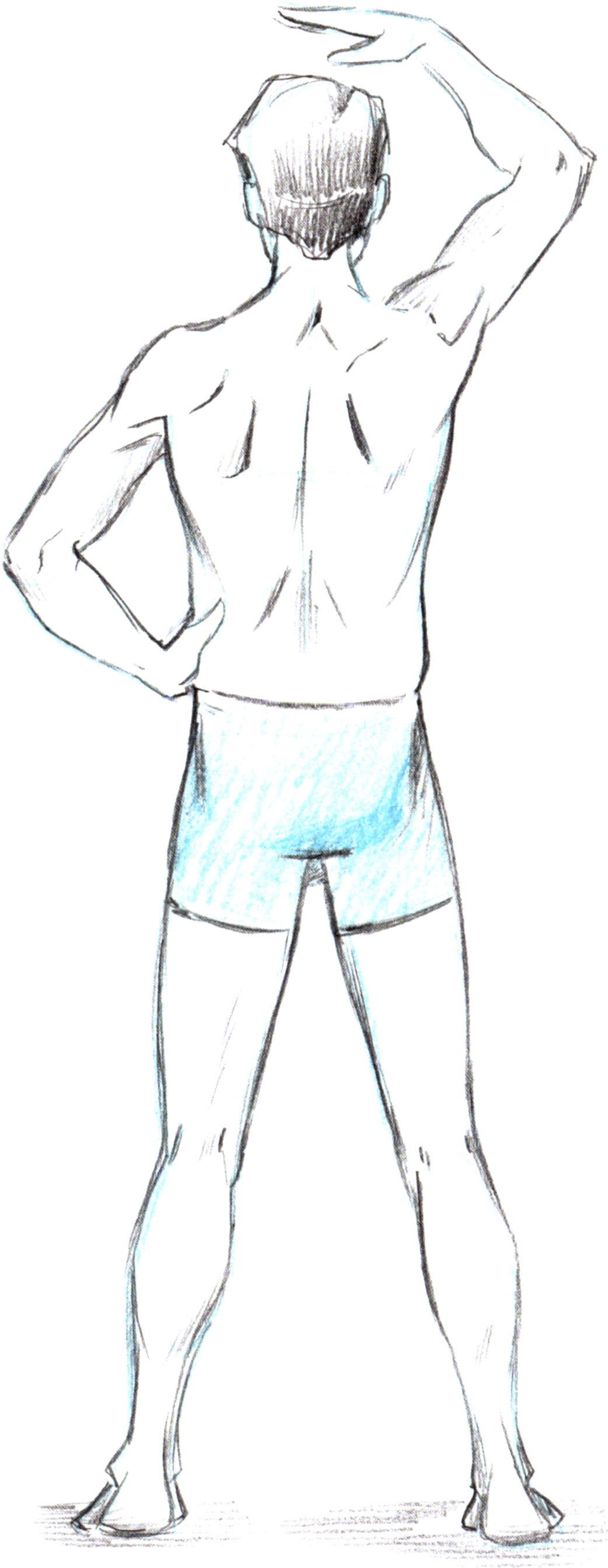

F) The shoulder muscle overlaps the upper arm muscles.

G) The shoulder muscle also overlaps the upper back.

H) These lines increase the definition of the lower back muscles or latissimus dorsi.

I) The torso has slightly extra mass at the bottom of the waist (I know this all too well!)

# POSES

While figure drawing is based on an understanding of the construction of the human body, it is also about effectively drawing the body in different positions. And so we now turn our attention to drawing a variety of poses.

A) Shoulder tilt adds dynamism.
B) Straight leg
C) Inward bend at the knee
D) Point toe outward.

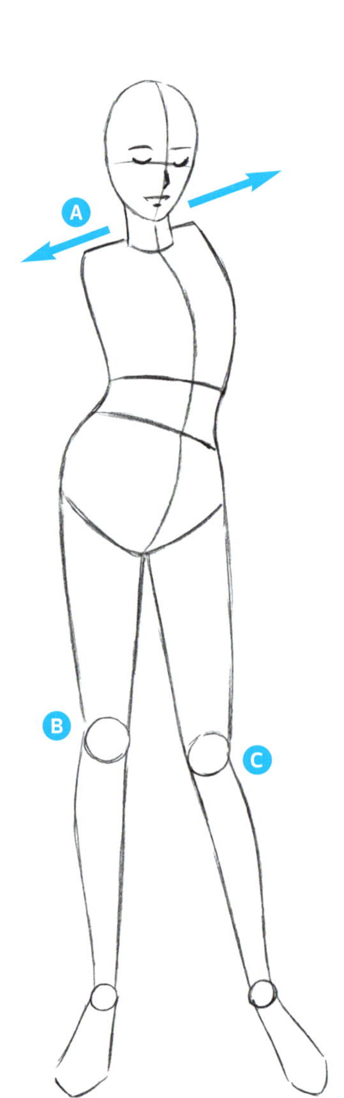


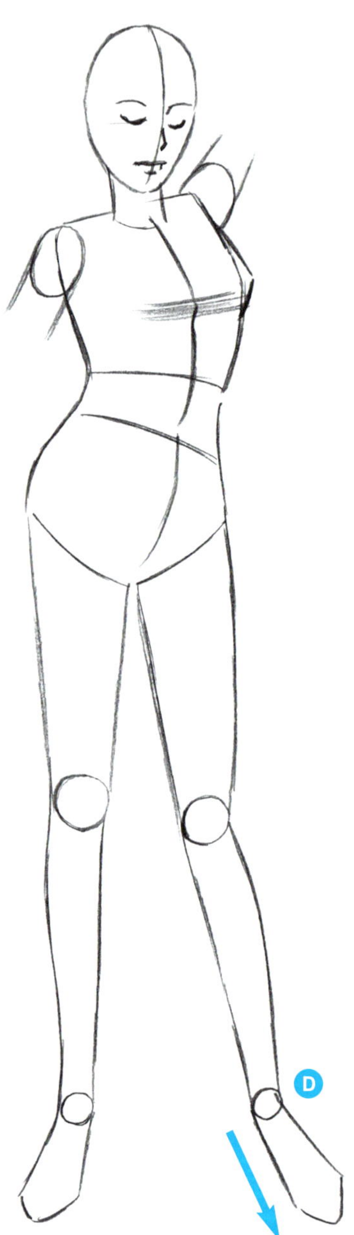


# POSE WITH BODY DYNAMICS

One of the easiest ways to add interest to a pose is by creating a significant shift in the angle of the shoulders. In this pose, the shoulders dip to the left. Adding to the asymmetry of the pose, one leg is straight, and positioned directly under the body (bearing most of the weight), while the other leg is bent and positioned away from the body.

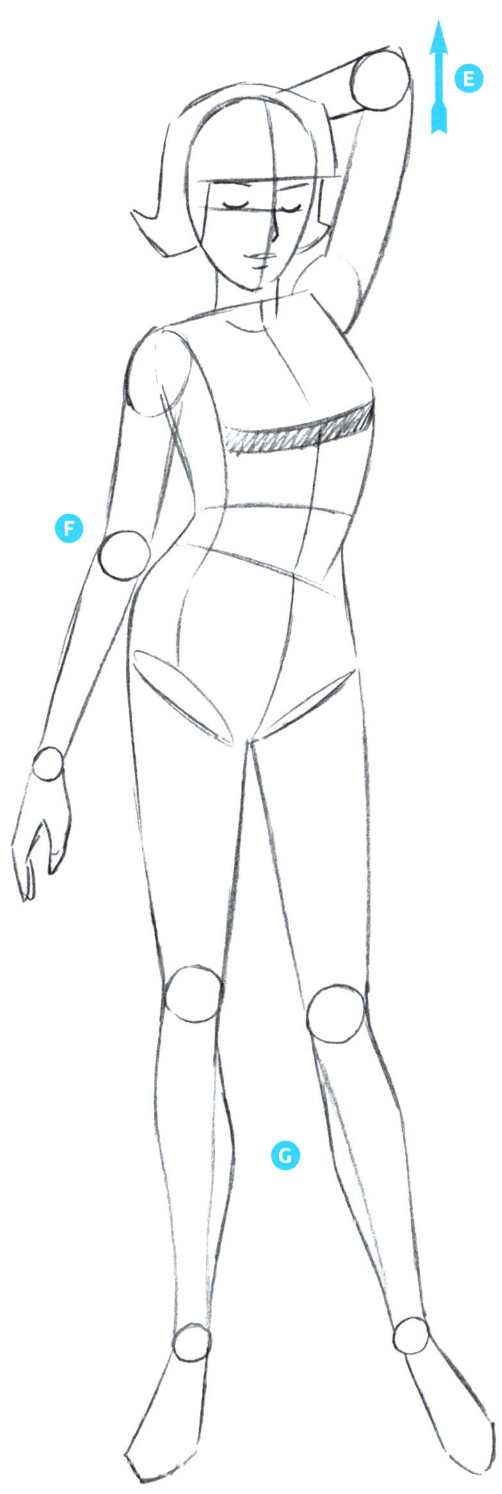


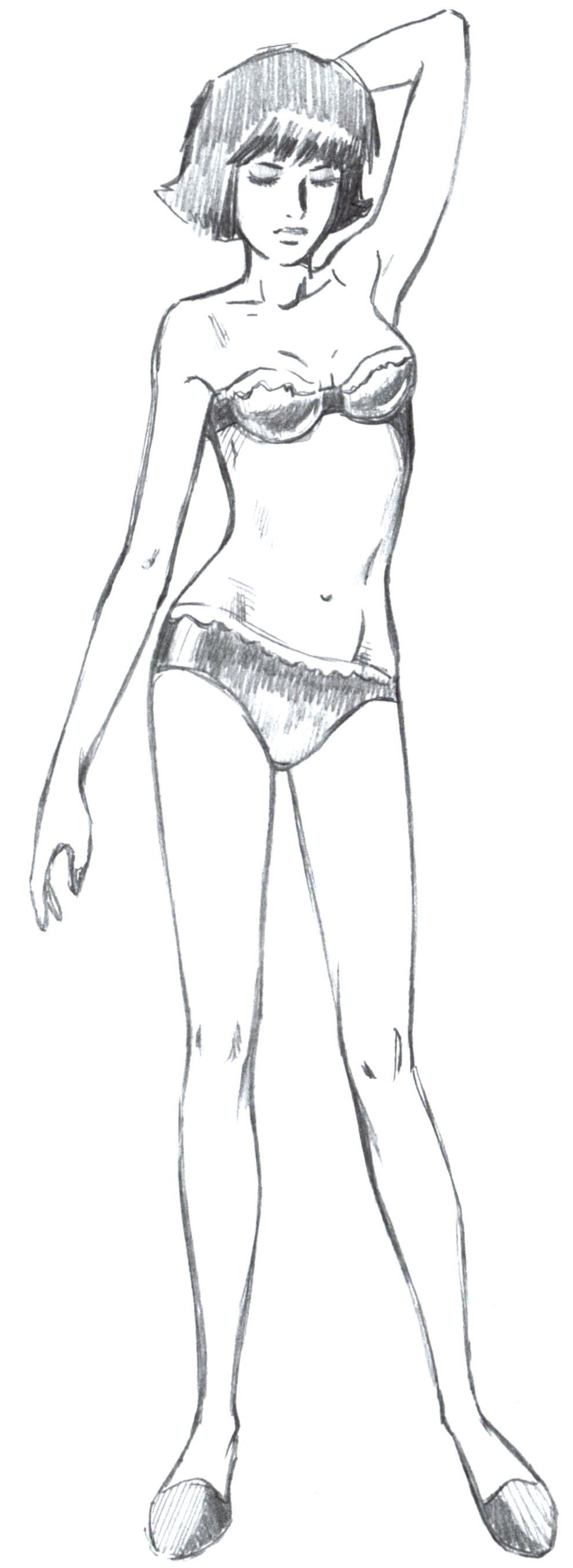

E) Elbow points upward.
F) Elbow bends slightly inward.
G) Add contours to the inner calves.

# THE THREE-QUARTER STANDING POSE

The challenge in drawing the three-quarter angle is to create the illusion of depth. Therefore, the near side of the figure is larger, while the far side is compressed. Let's take a look at how this plays out.

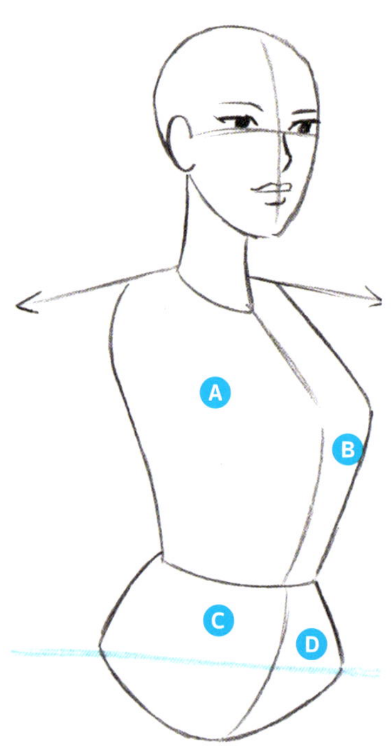


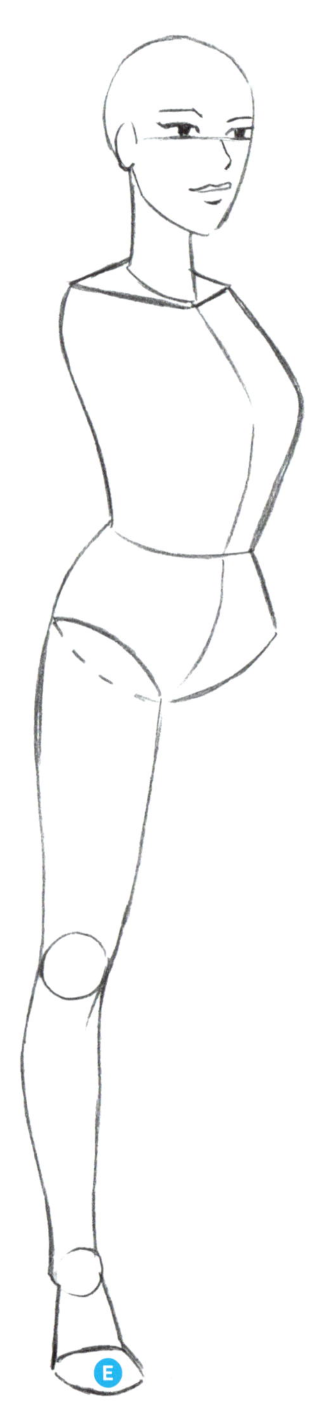


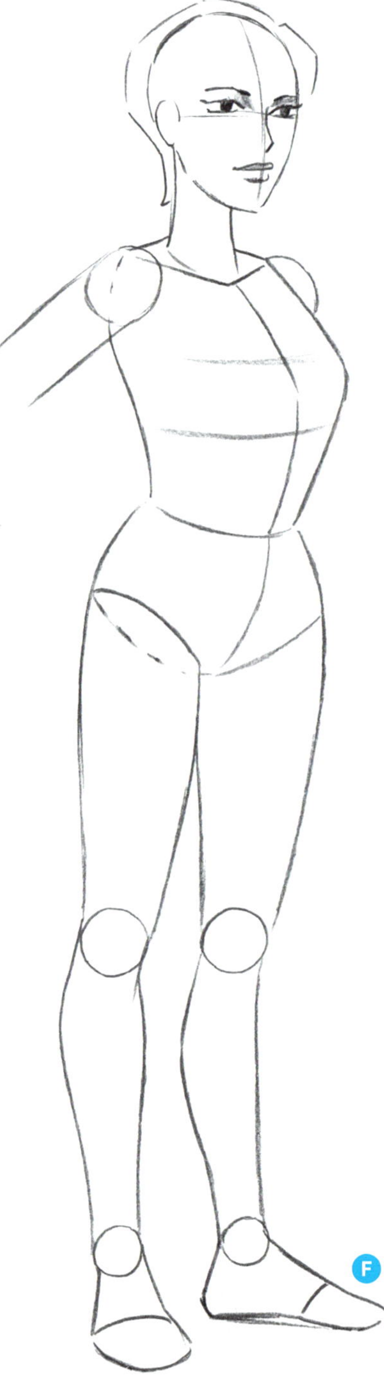


A) Larger side (upper body)
B) Compressed side (upper body)
C) Larger side (hips)
D) Compressed side (hips)
E) The near leg is slightly longer, and the foot points toward us.
F) The far leg is slightly shorter, and the foot points to the side.

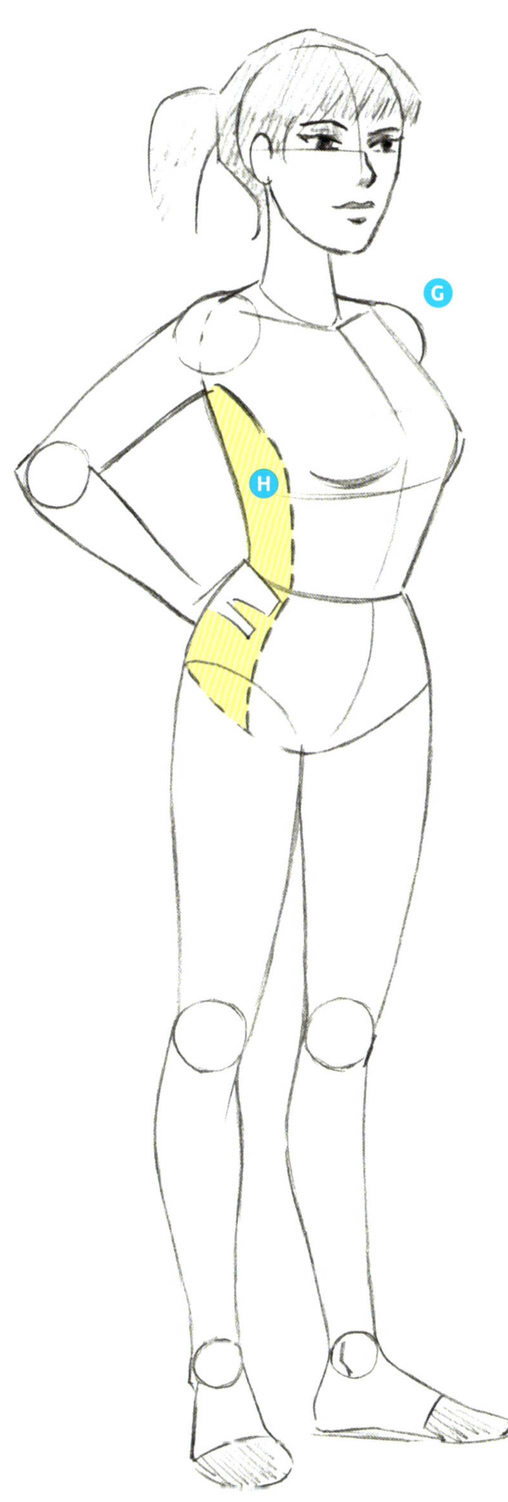


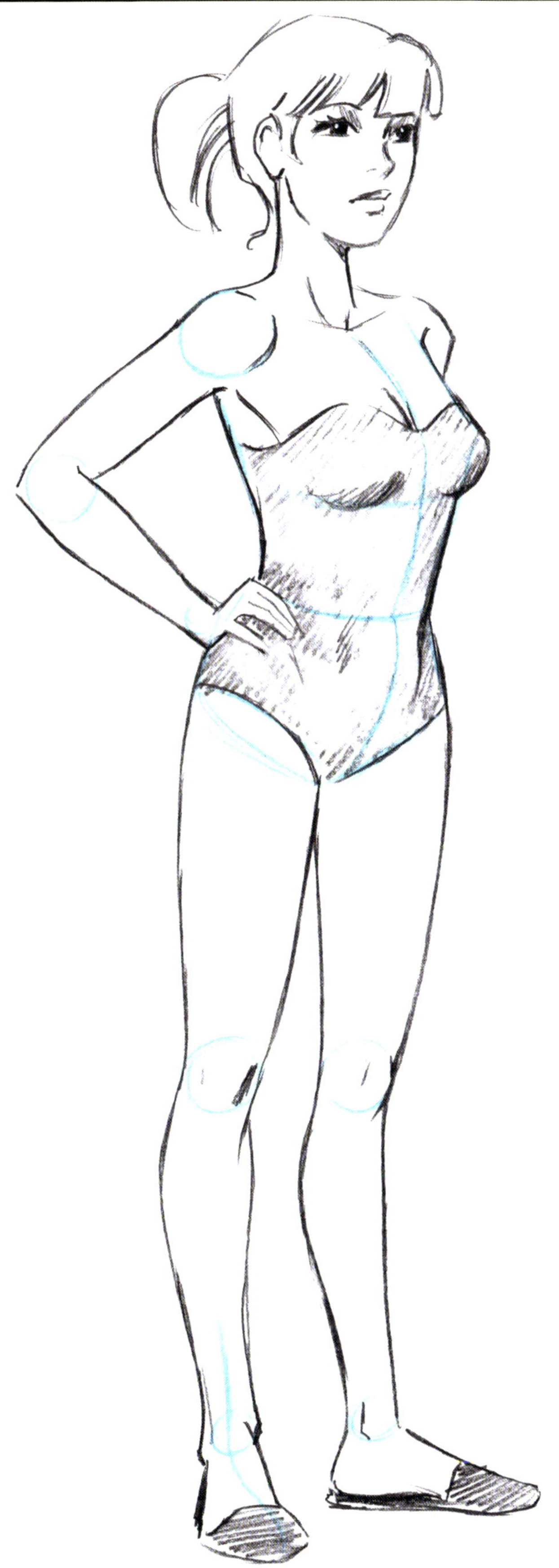

G) In the three-quarter view, the far shoulder may be visible, which adds to the look of depth.

H) The three-quarter view creates a "side plane" on the figure.

# BE INVENTIVE!

If you're drawing a figure in a side pose, bring your creativity to the pose. By individualizing a pose, you lift, stretch, and flex the muscles in interesting ways, which you can articulate by showing more definition. Creative poses can also emphasize different angles and sweeping lines.

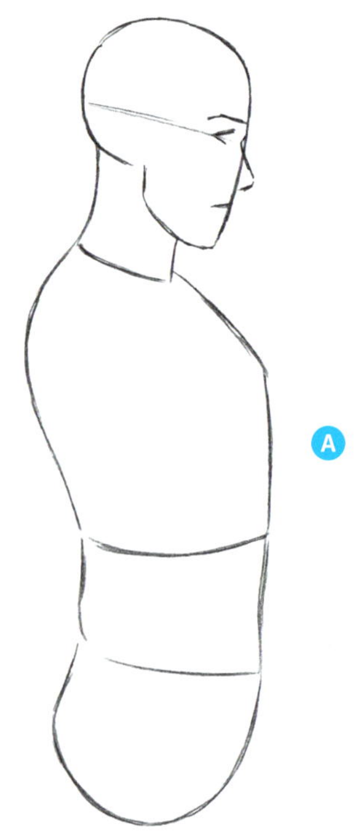

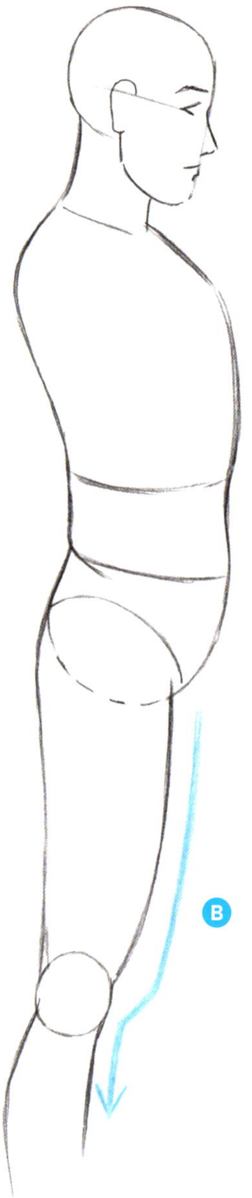

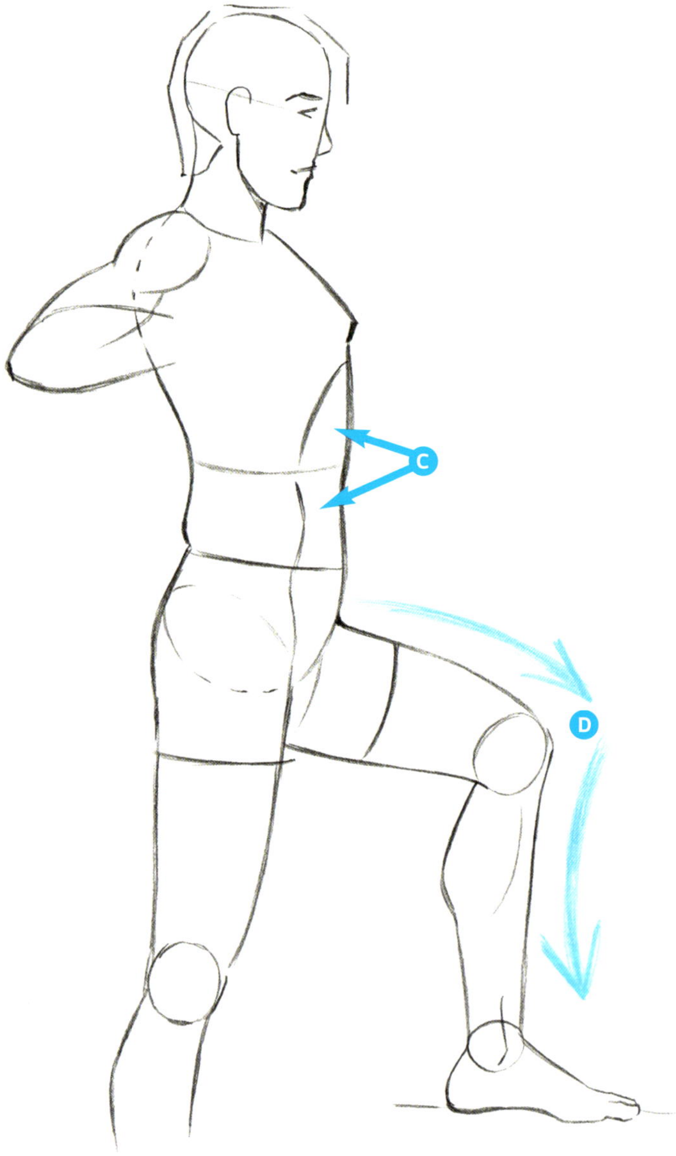

A) Start with an ordinary side pose for the upper half of the figure.

B) When the leg is bearing most of the body weight, the lower leg is indented.

C) Because the arms are pulled back, the torso experiences "stretch," which causes the articulation of the ribcage and abdominal wall.

D) Note the sweeping lines of the raised leg.

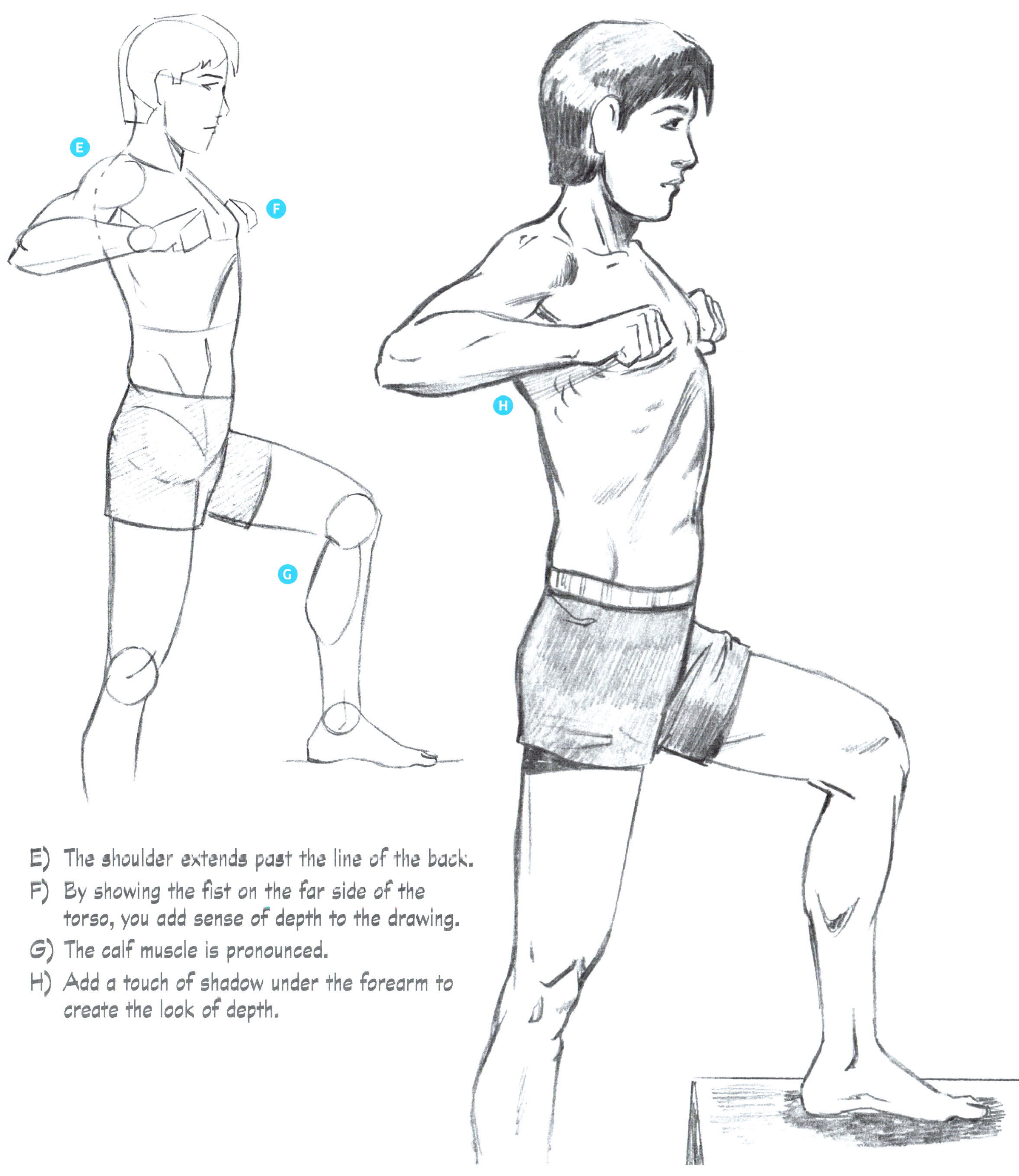


E) The shoulder extends past the line of the back.

F) By showing the fist on the far side of the torso, you add sense of depth to the drawing.

G) The calf muscle is pronounced.

H) Add a touch of shadow under the forearm to create the look of depth.

# THE THREE-QUARTER SEATED POSE

When you draw a figure in a sitting pose, you will naturally be concentrating on the legs, hips, and buttocks. But let's not overlook the torso, which still benefits from being drawn with a flowing Center Line. You get the best effect when a pose incorporates all of the body's dynamics working in unison.

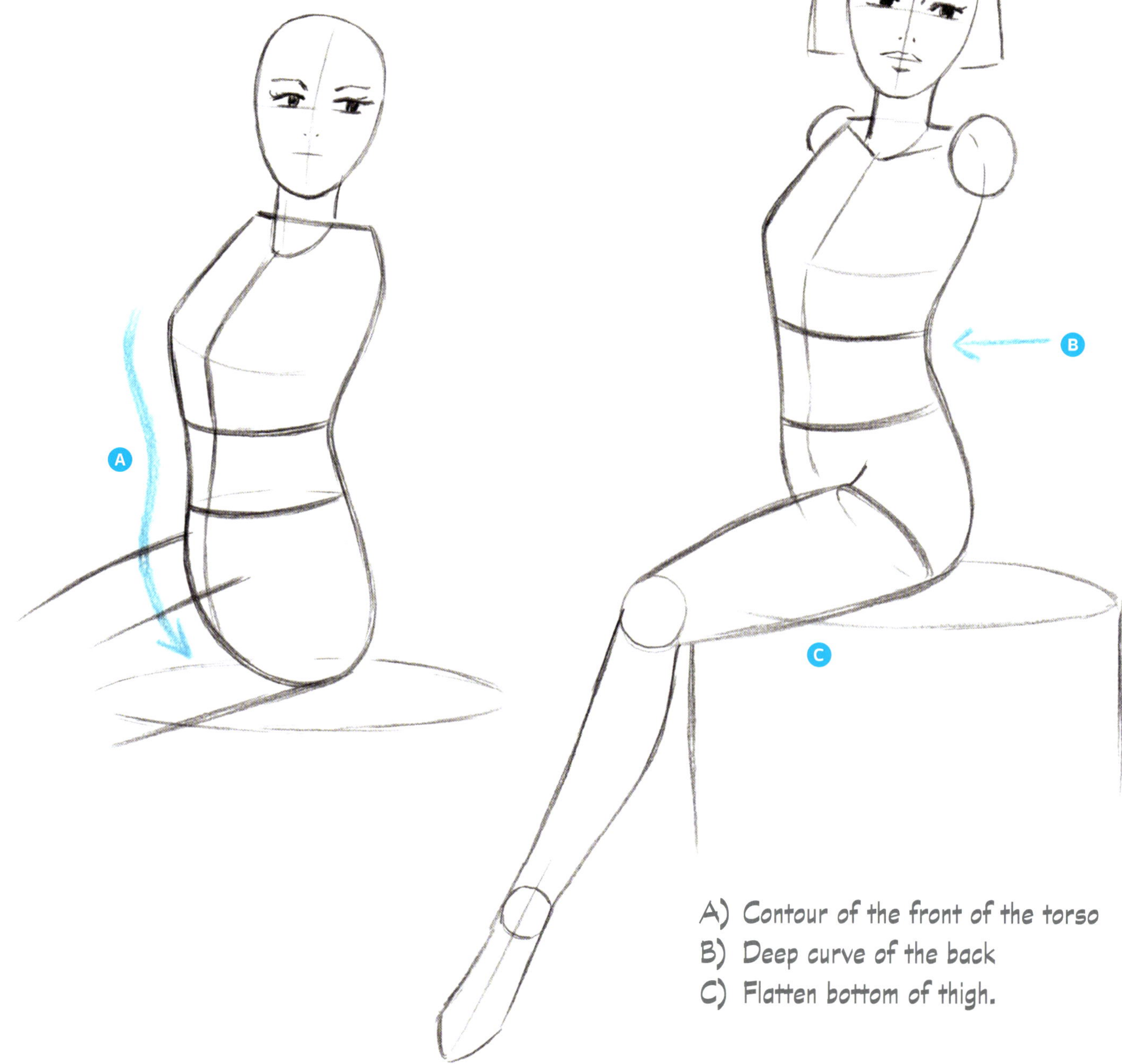


A) Contour of the front of the torso
B) Deep curve of the back
C) Flatten bottom of thigh.

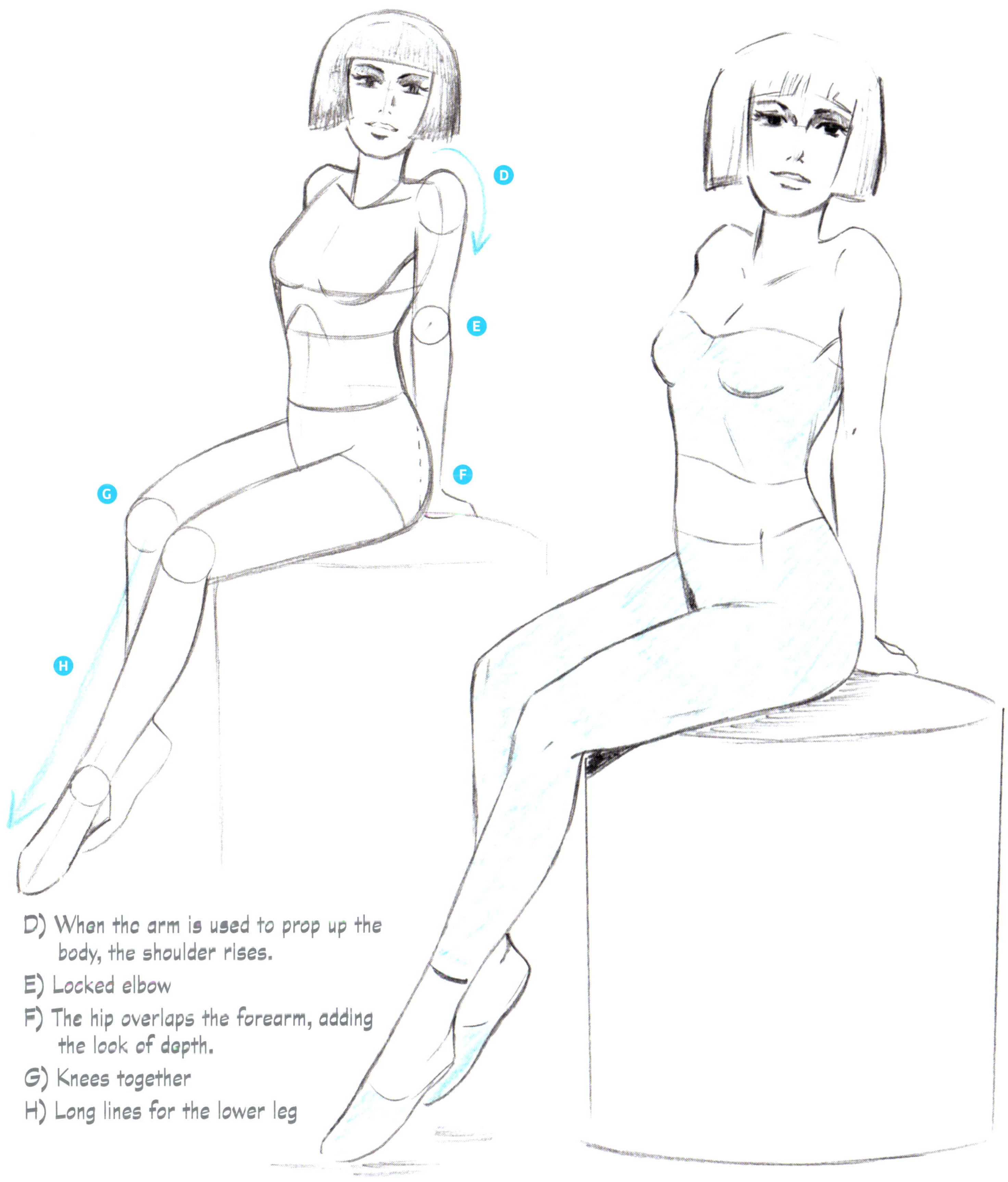


D) When the arm is used to prop up the body, the shoulder rises.

E) Locked elbow

F) The hip overlaps the forearm, adding the look of depth.

G) Knees together

H) Long lines for the lower leg

# USING PERSPECTIVE IN DRAWING THE FIGURE

We can use perspective as a tool with which to heighten the drama of a pose. Notice how the directional lines (horizontal arrows) tend to converge toward the middle of the figure (waistline). By drawing the body along these perspective guidelines, you increase the length of the body to the left of the Center Line, and shorten the body to the right of the center line. Although the effect is subtle, it is still perceived by the viewer, who experiences the figure as having a greater presence.

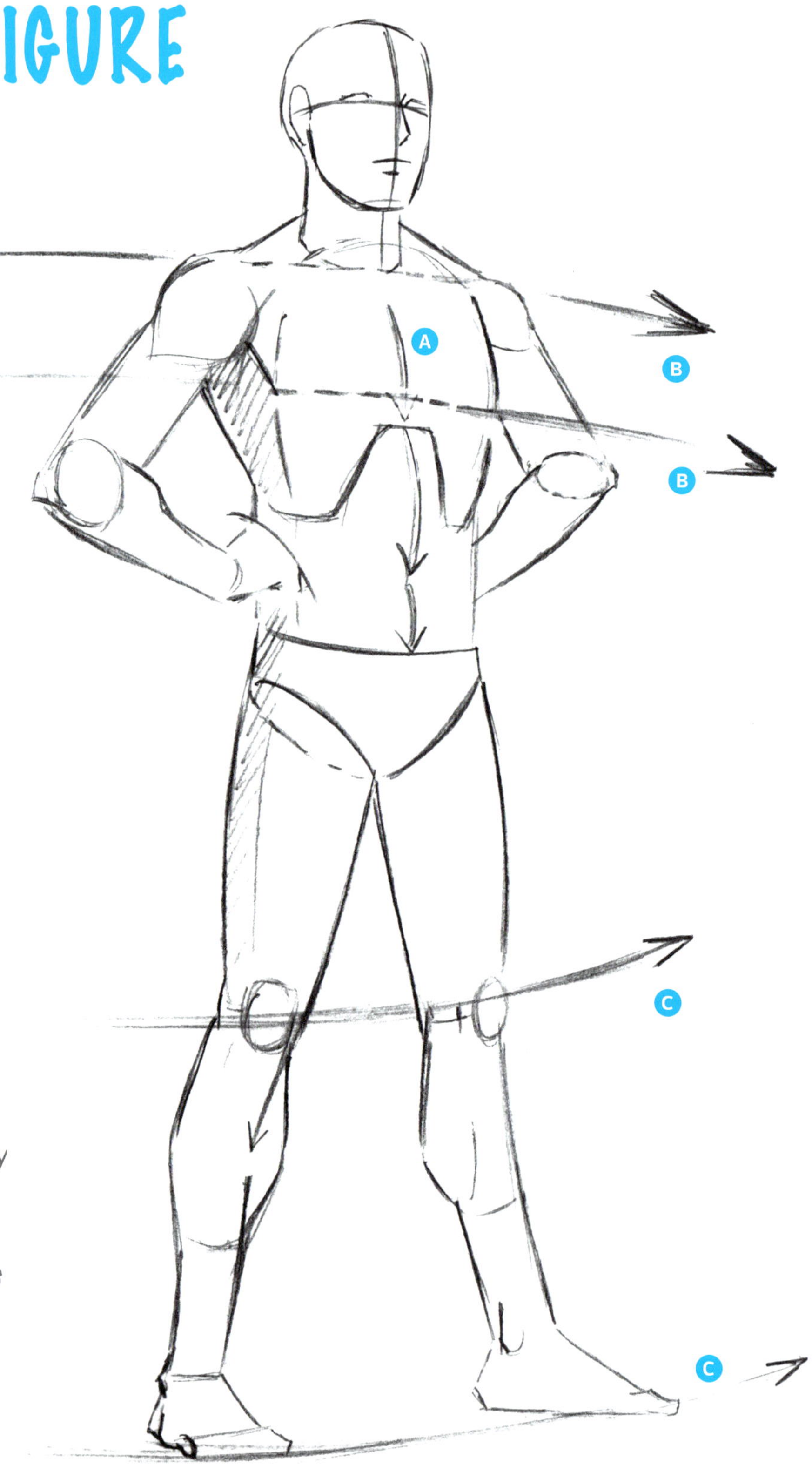


A) Center Line

B) The upper body slopes slightly downward along perspective guidelines.

C) The lower body lifts along the perspective guidelines.